Copyright @2021 by GREG RUEDIGER

All rights reserved. No part of this book may be reproduced in any form or by any electronic or mechanical means, including information storage and retrieval systems, without permission in writing from the publisher, except by reviewers, who may quote brief passages in a review.

This publication contains the opinions and ideas of its author. It is intended to provide helpful and informative material on the subjects addressed in the publication. The author and publisher specifically disclaim all responsibility for any liability, loss or risk, personal or otherwise, which is incurred as a consequence, directly or indirectly, of the use and application of any of the contents of this book.

WORKBOOK PRESS LLC
187 E Warm Springs Rd,
Suite B285, Las Vegas, NV 89119, USA

Website:	https://workbookpress.com/
Hotline:	1-888-818-4856
Email:	admin@workbookpress.com

Ordering Information:
Quantity sales. Special discounts are available on quantity purchases by corporations, associations, and others. For details, contact the publisher at the address above.

ISBN-13:   978-1-957618-02-9 (Paperback Version)
              978-1-957618-03-6 (Digital Version)

REV. DATE: 1.24.2022

EMOTIONAL POLLUTION

Always Present But Rarely Discussed

Greg Ruediger

To Beckie

ACKNOWLEDGEMENTS

The author would like to acknowledge those who participated in shaping the book. Special recognition is given to Joshua Smith, Freddie Johnson, Hugh Casey, Hudson Lazenby and Jeff Waller. Additionally, all individuals known and unknown whom he has directly or indirectly interacted with are recognized.

CONTENTS

Introduction 7

Chapter 1
    Emotional Pollution 10

Chapter 2
    Emotional Pollution Outcomes 39

Chapter 3
    Words 69

Chapter 4
    Propaganda 90

Chapter 5
    Measuring Emotional Pollution 116

Chapter 6
    Ideas to Offset Emotional Pollution 146

Content Review 182

References 184

Introduction

The beautiful blue skies are filled with soft billowing white clouds. The birds are chirping merrily as squirrels' race from one tree to another locating and gathering food for the long winter ahead. These and images like the pretty colors reflecting off a lake or dogs playing in the backyard often create feelings of warmth, joy and happiness. A sense of hope and optimism is sometimes also felt when looking at pictures, videos and listening to music. Beauty is all around us each moment of every day. In spite of this, people seldom notice it, or when they do, it is only for a brief moment. Instead, most are fearful, worrying how they will survive in a world perceived as insensitive to them. This observation is the focus of the book, *Emotional Pollution: Always Present but Rarely Discussed*.

Three major beliefs guide the writing of the book. One is people are inherently good. Yet, their actions at times have unintended negative outcomes. Second, a variety of perspectives on human behavior is needed. As other points of view are presented, critical accounts of individuals and events are sometimes necessary. However, it is not the intent of the author to be pessimistic, but rather to share ideas. Some of which might stimulate future scientific studies improving the quality of life. Lastly, information about emotional pollution may help readers uncover something they have not thought about before. This creates new opportunities for them to identify personal characteristics and societal variables affecting their level of happiness. If collective happiness would increase, positive energy may become more readily available to address some of the problems in the world today.

The book contains six chapters. Chapter 1 introduces the

concept of emotional pollution. It is defined as the innate, environmental or combination of elements negatively affecting thoughts and actions. Emotional pollution hinders the ability to live in the moment. Instead, people spend a lot of time thinking about the past or worrying about the future. With that being the case, emitting emotional pollution normally helps them feel better. Those affected then exhibit similar types of behavior to overcome their discomfort and pain. A number of outcomes result from this always present but rarely discussed emotional pollution cycle. Chapter 2 focuses on some of them. For individuals, frequent and intense emotional pollution may cause parts of the brain to be underdeveloped. This creates difficulties with memory, language and motor function. As these inabilities surface in daily activities, many adults adopt a norm-referenced perspective in which they determine their value or worth in comparison to others. A number of things happen when this occurs. Most of which represent an individual or groups attempt to gain something in order to feel a sense of contentment. This ongoing search leads to many different types of emotional pollution.

Chapter 3 explores the link between words and emotional pollution. The more subjective a terms definition, the greater likelihood misunderstandings result in pollutants. Individuals as well frequently use words to "mask" or "cover up" feelings and ideas in order to be a part of some desired group. As this evolves, adults focus mainly on themselves rather than on others. This is the reason why many well-intentioned actions perpetuate rather than lessen the difficulties associated with issues like extreme hunger, violence and inequality. Words also play a role in propaganda. A form of emotional pollution discussed in Chapter 4. Propaganda is subconscious or conscious actions by an individual or group to shape behavior. This fear-based strategy often results in children and adults conforming in order to be a part of a group. By willingly doing so, many gain a sense of acceptance while at the same time losing some degree of control over the events occurring in their life. When realizing that, a negative rather than positive mood makes it difficult to determine the truth. This leads to vast amounts of emotional pollution as information enters consciousness only to the degree it affects someone's sense of well-being. Propagandists also manipulate the use and meaning of words to create an atmosphere of discontent. The term *happiness* is an example. For many, an ongoing dilemma exists as to what it feels like. Without clarity and certainty in definition, adults are more vulnerable to believe things without much thought. Emotional pollution is the natural outcome.

Chapter 5 describes how to measure emotional pollution. Guiding the systematic data collection process is the belief that emotional pollution affects need fulfilment, moods; and, ultimately happiness. More specifically, the self-awareness activity consists of the RYB Color Wheel, numbers and a personal journal. Colors and their assigned numbers represent an individual's mood. The higher the rating, the more likely a person's needs are met; and, a sense of happiness is felt. An Emotional Pollution Perception Scale is used to identify experiences influencing the daily rating. As information is gathered, emotional pollution plans of action are sometimes developed. Chapter 6 provides ideas to consider in the design of these life-alternating documents. Some of the topics discussed are emotional literacy, communication, acceptance and personal identity. Individual and collective change is more likely to occur when people become aware of emotional pollution. A societal constant rarely discussed.

Chapter 1
Emotional Pollution

Environmental pollution is an issue of concern as countries become more industrialized. As individuals consume rather than produce goods they are often unaware of how their actions affect the environment. An example in China is how citizens are purchasing automobiles emitting toxins rather than relying on bicycles for transportation. As this cultural shift unfolds, news accounts graphically portray poor air quality and the importance of wearing masks to prevent certain substances from entering the body. Another related development is how advancements in technology have made it more cost-effective to use hydraulic fracturing in the oil and natural gas industry. These new procedures have created a variety of employment opportunities while at the same time negatively effecting the environment. In response to these and other complex environmental issues, countries throughout the World have created agencies to monitor soil, water and air quality. One such organization is the United States Environmental Protection Agency.

The Environmental Protection Agency (EPA) attempts to protect human health and the environment. According to its Website, the EPA's purpose is to ensure that:

- all Americans are protected from significant risks to human health and the environment where they live, learn and work;
- national efforts to reduce environmental risk are based on the best available scientific information;

- federal laws protecting human health and the environment are enforced fairly and effectively;
- environmental protection is an integral consideration in United States policies concerning natural resources, human health, economic growth, energy, transportation, agriculture, industry and international trade, and these factors are similarly considered in establishing environmental policy;
- all parts of society – communities, individuals, businesses, and state, local and tribal governments – have access to accurate information sufficient to effectively participate in managing human health and environmental risks;
- environmental protection contributes to making our communities and ecosystems diverse, sustainable and economically productive; and the United States plays a leadership role in working with other nations to protect the global environment (United States Environmental Protection Agency, 2014).

United States citizens continue to alter the environment in many different ways. For example, some local zoning ordinances have resulted in black bears foraging for food and shelter in local neighborhoods. In many other situations, children and adults continue to throw garbage on the ground. Even the once pristine springs of Florida have been harmed by septic tank and fertilizer run-off. In spite of these obvious challenges, individual and collective actions to protect the environment have had limited success. This reality of life is not new but rather reflects the ongoing emotion-based struggle to obtain a balance between conservation and human consumption.

Emotion: A Natural Form of Environmental Pollution

Another less tangible form of environmental pollution is linked to human emotion. Human emotions are sensations that naturally occur within a person. They range from primitive reflexes and responses to multifaceted complexities described and labeled as happiness, anger, joy, sadness, guilt, hope, love and a variety of other terms. These internal feelings vary for each individual and present themselves on a frequency and intensity continuum. For example, when someone has an experience, visual and auditory stimuli trigger to some degree an instinctive response. Initially, this is reflected in a baby's cry for comfort and ultimately ends at the mourning of life. In between these periods, varying degrees of emotion are present in each experience. It is also clear nonverbal and verbal communication patterns convey human emotion. The most primitive or basic example is a person's voice tone and the intensity associated with a given message (whisper/yell). On the opposite end of the emotional spectrum are art forms capturing human feelings through song lyrics, poetry, paintings and other means of expression.

Human survival instincts cause negative emotions to dominate positive. As these difficult feelings arise, emotional discomfort usually triggers to some degree an autonomic nervous system response. This results in someone experiencing increased adrenalin, heart rate and level of arousal. A recent example occurred when an athlete was running on a desolate dirt road. Despite traveling the same route for years, something different happened that day. While on mile number five, a group of dogs began running after him. His body responded by changing temperature, heart rate and energy level in order to get away. Of course, a pack of animals chasing someone is extreme; nevertheless, emotion-led behavior is present everywhere. Emotions as well appear to act paradoxically; they help individuals protect themselves, while at other times they create a sense of uneasiness.

Variables Influencing Emotion

A persons' genetic endowment provides the foundation for emotion. Emotions are therefore more likely to occur in certain individuals rather than others. For some, anger and shame are common while others seem happy and joyful. An important question to consider though is what environmental variables increase the likelihood children and adults experience certain emotions. As one might expect, an individual's family plays a significant role in determining the frequency and intensity of feelings. In particular, parenting styles influence internal sensations (Baumrind, 1991). For example, authoritative parents provide rules and discuss reasons for them. Young people in these types of families usually exhibit positive emotions associated with self-motivation, assertiveness and the ability to work productively with others. Authoritarian parents on the other hand, promote negative emotions by establishing rules to be blindly obeyed. This parenting approach promotes a lack of closeness and empowerment while at the same time fostering resentment between the child and parent. Permissive parents also provide little emotional support as they allow their children to decide almost everything, like what to eat, wear, and when to go to bed. Kids living in this situation are markedly less assertive and usually lack fundamental emotional understanding. Similarly, rejecting-neglecting parents are non-supportive of their children's goals and activities; their lack of parenting may actively promote negative emotions (Baumrind, 1991). Siblings and extended family members also play a role in the development of emotions. To think further about families and emotions, a continuum beginning with calmness ending with upheaval might be helpful. From this conceptualization, one could suggest, if a child's parents spend the majority of time closer to upheaval than calmness, they are more likely to model and reinforce negative emotions.

The education system also shapes emotion. In a traditional classroom, children have limited opportunities to learn about emotion. Rather, they are relatively passive as the teacher does most of the talking while students spend time at their desks listening, responding when called on and completing assigned tasks. Student progress is determined by how well they perform on a uniform set of standards for their grade. The Every Student Succeeds Act (2015) reinforces this instructional approach by expecting states to develop standardized reading and mathematics examinations. If students do not meet yearly skill development requirements, school districts might face sanctions. A natural outcome of this policy decision is that many teachers feel powerless, as they cannot veer from the scripted curriculum. If they do so, some may be in danger of receiving a poor evaluation and eventually lose their job. Educators as well are expected to teach large amounts of information in a relatively short time. This quantity rather than quality mindset has resulted in many being unable to model or even discuss the characteristics associated with emotional literacy. Another education reality is, in some school districts students have limited exposure to content areas not measured on standardized tests. This narrow approach to curriculum and learning may oppress rather than nurture emotional growth.

Changes in the school culture have resulted from another educational trend: the inclusion movement. In inclusive schools and classrooms, emphasis is placed on building communities with everyone's gifts and talents recognized and utilized to the fullest extent possible (Turnbull, Turnbull, Wehmeyer & Shogren, 2020). Each individual is thought of as a worthwhile member of the group who has a role to play in supporting others to foster self-esteem, pride in peer accomplishment, mutual respect, and a sense of belonging. In spite of this well-intentioned philosophy, two negative consequences result; class sizes become larger and vast learning differences exist between students. To offset these challenges, special and regular education professionals work in collaboration to design learning opportunities that are sensitive to all learners (Friend & Bursuck, 2019). This change in professional roles, and the constantly evolving learning environment, creates a great deal of anxiety and confusion among students and education professionals. As this unfolds, fear rather than joy often creates an atmosphere of "just trying to survive." This mindset usually results in little emphasis placed on teaching students about emotion.

The media also affects emotions. The characteristics of those portrayed in television shows, athletic events and news accounts often act as role models. Evidence of this is sometimes noticed when talking with adolescent boys. When you ask them, "what do you want to do when you grow up?" In many instances, they say, "I want to be a football or basketball player." Media messages also influence adults. A person's identity and emotional well-being is often based on some standard conveyed through the media. For many, a certain type of car or home is an indicator they are doing well. Statements such as, "he must be alright, he is driving a Lexus isn't he, or he has a vacation home," illuminate this way of thinking. Despite the obvious impact of commercials, news stories as well have an effect on shaping emotions. The way information is presented and the length of time it is in the news cycle determines how viewers interpret the events. In the United States for example, recent school shootings have acted as a catalyst to discuss a multitude of emotion-based issues such as access to guns and mental health.

In summary, a person's genetic endowment provides the basis for how they feel and act. Experiences within the family, school and information from the media influence these innate internal sensations to some degree. This begins with the type and frequency of interaction between an infant and their care provider. As children become older, parenting styles along with what is learned in school and through the media act in some way to shape emotions. It is also clear that emotions act paradoxically; they provide a sense of safety for some while at the same time creating difficulties for others. This reality of the human condition highlights the complexities of human emotion and the pollution associated with it.

Emotional Pollution

Emotional pollution is the innate, environmental or combination of elements negatively affecting thoughts and actions. This idea is based on the link between emotion and the brains ability to adapt its structure and wiring (neuroplasticity) in response to environmental stimuli. More precisely, an individuals' behavior reflects their neurological identity at a given point in time. For instance, if Jim perceives something coming towards him, his actions to move away or get closer to the object reflects the complex activities occurring within his brain. This multifaceted evolving process helps Jim lessen discomfort while often simultaneously creating difficulties for those around him. An example might be his parenting style. When frustrated with his son, Jim's threats to take away the car keys may make him feel better; it ultimately though may adversely affect his relationship.

The concept of emotional pollution can be described through a simple exercise. To begin, close your eyes and be as physically still as possible. Then, try to reach a state of being where no feelings or thoughts arise and enter into consciousness. Once reaching this point, determine how long it took to get there, and the length of time in which you remain. For some, it might not be possible to reach a state of calmness, for others, the duration is very short. The reason for this is emotional pollution triggers to some degree basic survival instincts. As this occurs, fear influences thoughts and actions. As a result, individuals are more likely to perceive others as being insensitive and disrespectful to them. Some examples today are political leaders viewed as not understanding their constituents, the rich having little idea what it is like to be poor or men not being aware of the needs of women. These negative feelings contribute to, and at times, cause personal and societal problems.

Another example of emotional pollution occurs when Betty decides to walk her dog Bruno. When putting on her shoes she does not realize a small rock is in her right shoe. She starts walking and notices that her foot feels different; yet, she does not stop. In spite of the discomfort, Betty is enjoying Bruno and the lovely scenery along the trail. As she continues on the two-mile trek, the feeling in her foot begins to create pain. She also starts to experience less enjoyment because some of her energy is now focused on her foot rather than Bruno and the pretty leaves on the trees along the roadway. When reflecting upon this, if Betty would have stopped immediately and removed the rock, she possibly would have had a more pleasant walk. She also would not have the lingering effects associated with discomfort and pain. Perhaps one could further conclude the simplicity of this example does not truly capture the depth of emotional pollution; rather, it is an attempt to associate a real-life experience with an abstract notion. Therefore, to clarify, emotional pollution is broader than John Maynard Keynes animal spirts theory. His ideas focused on how the performance of economic markets is largely determined by mental processes (Akerlof & Shiller, 2009). Some of which are not rational. Instead, emotions associated with belief and trust; and, ultimately confidence influences how individuals and groups invest their money. Market fluctuations and volatilities are examples of emotional pollution. Emotional pollution however is present in all cultural contexts.

Characteristics of Emotional Pollution

People respond to environmental stimuli in a variety of ways. Yet, no two individuals react consistently to persons, places and things. Instead, genetic and experiential differences cause them to develop their own unique perspective of the world around them. As this multifaceted, dynamic process evolves, survival instincts and the human ego act as catalysts for the creation and emission of emotional pollution. This is reflected in various types and degrees of autonomic nervous system responses. The autonomic nervous system is comprised of the sympathetic system, which is the "fight or flight mechanism"; and, the parasympathetic system is a sense of physiological balance and calmness (Siegel, 2010). In the sympathetic system, large amounts of energy are expended in response to increased adrenalin, heart rate and level of arousal. As individuals experience this, they are more likely to encounter challenges in life ranging from physical ailments to difficulties in personal relationships. However, once obtaining a sense of personal safety, they gradually transition into the parasympathetic system. When that occurs, emotional pollution becomes more abstract, consisting of a variety of interrelated characteristics evolving within a complex, dynamic culture.

Discomfort and pain are the feelings associated with emotional pollution. As children and adults encounter these uncomfortable internal sensations, they normally act in ways to help them feel better. While doing so, they frequently create difficulties for others. In response, those affected then exhibit similar behavior. This emotional pollution cycle is context and situation specific. For most adults, certain environments are more comfortable than others are. An example is a place of employment. If someone has worked for the same company a long time, they know the daily routines. These predictable patterns of behavior provide a sense of emotional safety. In contrast, a new employees' anxiety often causes them to be vulnerable to emotional pollution. For instance, if a co-worker tells a joke they are likely to think it is about them when in fact it is not. At a more abstract level, any threat to the new employees' ego is perceived as emotional pollution. This is evident when thinking about how someone normally reacts to a reprimand by his or her boss. In most cases, if it takes place in a private rather than public setting, the person feels discomfort for a shorter period of time. Nevertheless, if the employer frequently reprimands, a culture of fear naturally results. When this happens, emotional pollution is usually widespread because employees are concerned about losing their job. Regardless of the environment, if people are involved, emotional pollution is present.

Communication is a major feature of emotional pollution. The most obvious example is word selection. Words reflect three distinct emotion-based categories: (1) neutral (2) positive and (3) negative. Neutral words consist of *such, how, as, when, where, is, begin, after, daily* and certain names of objects. A sample of positive terms includes *helpful, happy, benefit, advantage, significant, wonderful, splendid, joyful, colorful,* and *abundant*. Negative terms are *sorry, sad, problem, harm, disillusionment, overwhelmed, depressed, frightened* and *troubled*. In most cases, children and adults use words reflecting their emotional well-being. As this happens, self-preservation in whatever form it presents itself triggers emotional pollution. For instance, the term *problem* invokes a variety of negative images and responses. In others, some perceive it as opportunities to learn. These differences in perspective result in various forms of pollutants that divide rather than unite individuals and groups. Another related communication issue is voice tone. In some situations, the listener thinks the person is yelling at them or is angry when that is not the case. Individuals then try to change the topic or end the conversation in order to escape the uncomfortable situation. This too though is a form of emotional pollution, as it does not promote the development and nurturing of interpersonal relationships.

The frequency and timing of emotional pollution determines its impact. For instance, a young person might reach a level of toxic stress if they consistently experience adverse childhood experiences. Once reaching this point, certain neurotransmitters in the brain may not develop or be strengthened to the extent needed to successfully participate in daily activities. As a result, discomfort and pain could make it difficult to rest. Without proper sleep, the mind and body struggle to detoxify and replenish for future experiences. When this happens, children and adults may not develop the biological foundation needed to offset and overcome the negative energy associated with emotional pollution. Instead, they disproportionally collect and distribute it. A simple illustration is a young girl playing with a plastic bucket at the beach. The amount of sand particles in her container represents the number of times emotional pollution has resulted to some degree in a lack of need fulfillment. While experiencing various people and events, the frequency and intensity of emotional pollution determines the number of particles in her bucket. For instance, if she is physically abused, large amounts are deposited. As the bucket begins to fill, her identity is being shaped. At certain points in time, what is in her bucket has more of an impact. Logically, the younger she is the greater the effect. Another important variable is the time required to fill her bucket. If at age twenty-one, it is quarter or half full, she will be more likely to feel positive about herself. In contrast, if the bucket has been filled many times prior to adulthood, she is going to struggle throughout life. These ongoing challenges may cause her to believe someone other than herself will determine what she experiences. She might also develop an ongoing sense of mistrust in others. This increases the chance of her becoming defensive, judgmental, opinionated and unwilling to accept those who are significantly different from her. As these personal characteristics develop and evolve, most of her actions will probably focus on obtaining a sense of safety and security. While doing so, she will create and emit large amounts of emotional pollution.

Emotional pollution also consists of less tangible characteristics. For instance, it perpetuates and strengthens the innate fear of the dark. This is the reason why streetlights exist and manufactures of hallway and bedroom night-lights continue to make money. From a cultural perspective, the survival instincts associated with darkness and ongoing emotional pollution is the reason why children and adults with black or brown skin are treated differently than those who are white. Of course, Caucasians will not openly admit it, but most are scared of individuals looking different from them. These uncomfortable feelings often lead to actions devaluing and ultimately dehumanizing people. Evidence of this is readily available in books describing the historical experiences of Native Americans and slaves. Even though this information is available, basic survival instincts and ongoing pollutants continue to act as the foundation for inequality and discrimination in the legal system, employment practices, educational opportunities, health care and a host of other social institutions. Emotional pollution not only contributes and reinforces these societal ills but also exists because of them.

Morality is another characteristic. When adults exhibit an action violating a person's beliefs, emotional pollution usually guides how they are treated. For example, many believe abortion is wrong. Those choosing to terminate life are often looked down-upon and even condemned by some for their decision. In response, statements like "Who are you to judge me?" "It is my body and I will do what I want with it" not only increase the amount of emotional pollution, but also fuel the intensity in which it exists. Other controversial issues contribute to the type and amount of emotional pollution present. A number of citizens for instance become disillusioned and even angry when observing the clearing of a wooded area to build a restaurant or gas station. These images coupled with ongoing thoughts of harming the environment frequently result in negative attitudes toward community decision-makers. Many of these feelings not only permeate those directly involved but also later contaminate the mood of others. Mood contagion certainly acts as an antecedent and ongoing catalyst for the creation and emission of emotional pollution.

Emotional pollution is present in various paradoxes. These contradictions occur in many different contexts. An example is religion. Throughout time, the Bible and Qur'an have been used to teach certain beliefs and actions perceived favorably by a higher power. If accepted as true, an afterlife will consist of entering the kingdom of heaven rather than the gates of hell. This faith in an ultimate being is used to answer questions not easily explained. For instance, it is common to hear, "it is part of God's plan" when someone experiences a tragedy. As an individuals' faith evolves and strengthens, they congregate with others having similar beliefs. This form of self-insulation provides a sense of acceptance and belonging while creating a number of unattended outcomes. The most obvious is the tendency to judge others. This sometimes results in public and private institutions developing policies and procedures insensitive to certain individuals and groups. Another related issue is associated with the phrase *moral compass*. It is difficult if not impossible to determine what acceptable behavior is when each religion has a variety of nuances, sub-streams, counter-streams, weaknesses, problems and minority opinions. Without a clear consensus, confusion often leads to disharmony and divisiveness among and between people. This form of negative energy acts as fuel to ignite and continue the emission of emotional pollution.

Judeo Christianity provides additional examples. One is how people should become more "Christ Like". This belief is based on interpretations of Biblical stories describing how children and adults should exhibit actions similar to Christ. By doing so, they will have a good life while on Earth and ultimately be perceived favorably in the afterlife. This way of thinking is impacted by the concepts of "free-will" and "sin". As imperfect beings (sinners), it is impossible for human beings truly to become like Christ. Rather, the gift of free-will leads to an ongoing struggle to obtain something that is impossible. As sinners, individuals are more likely then to perceive themselves and those around them in a negative light. This leads to many self-centered actions, many of which are emotional pollutants. In some ways, Christ could be considered cruel as people are taught to be more like him while at the same time he has given them certain abilities (normally, perceived as acts of love) which make it impossible to do so. Other, "Christ Like" contradictions are present in the Ten Commandments (English Standard Version, Bible, 2001, Ex. 20:2-17). For instance, the Sixth Commandment is thou shall not kill. How then can wars be justified? Why are soldiers considered heroes when they kill to protect their country? Answers to these difficult questions illuminate the complexities surrounding religious beliefs and emotional pollution.

Technology is another topic containing a variety of emotional pollution-based paradoxes. From a positive perspective, individuals historically denied opportunities now have increased access to information. For instance, regardless of time and place, college courses are available through a number of Internet platforms. Social media also helps adults rekindle past relationships. It too is a communication tool to organize and promote various collective actions such as, the Arab Spring and Occupy Wall Street movements. In spite of these positive societal gains, a number of other less beneficial outcomes arise because of emotional pollution. Some think they know more than they actually do about a particular subject. When that happens, many only read articles validating their currently held beliefs. This form of intellectual self-insulation provides personal validation while also increasing the likelihood of experiencing emotional pollution. Adults often then attain comfort by communicating with others who think and act similar to them. However, if that coping mechanism does not provide relief, many feel disenfranchised and silenced as they worry some person or system (government) has the power to take away something they value. Normally, this is their job and the lifestyle in which it provides. Another concern is how technology has changed human interactions. Some academics suggest the quantity and quality of personal relationships have been adversely affected by the amount of time children and adults interact with digital devices. With limited human contact, individuals and groups are less apt to be aware of those different from them. This leads to the ongoing emission of emotional pollution.

Another paradox is related to the production and manufacturing of goods. In many industries, new forms of technology have resulted in higher productivity levels at lower costs. Machines have caused many to lose their job as the need for manual labor has decreased. It too has created a situation where employees are required to develop new skill sets in order to obtain a job providing a livable wage. This workforce transition has drawn attention to another societal issue creating emotional pollution, the digital divide. Certain individuals are at an advantage because they have access and knowledge of various forms of technology while others do not. An example today is the way in which someone applies for a job. For most major employers, job seekers are required to complete an application online. Those having limited experience with technology would be at a significant disadvantage. For some, they may become so overwhelmed they do not apply. It simply is too confusing and frustrating. When that happens, adults are more likely to give up trying to improve their quality of life. Rather, they focus on just trying to survive in a world in which they perceive as insensitive to them.

In summary, the characteristics of emotional pollution consist of interconnected variables. From a biological point of view, the frequency and extent of emotional pollution is determined by an individual's autonomic nervous system response to environmental stimuli. Basic survival instincts to some degree govern this process. From a cultural perspective, feelings of discomfort and pain trigger the creation and emission of emotional pollution. As this multifaceted dynamic unfolds, an emotional pollution cycle develops in which individuals exhibit actions to help them feel better while simultaneously creating difficulties for others. Those affected then demonstrate similar actions. This sequence of events typically occurs within the context of communication, morality, and a host of other situations and settings. Emotional pollution also has less tangible characteristics. The most important perhaps is how it contributes to the innate fear of the dark. It too creates various paradoxes in religion, technology and manufacturing. These contradictions in thoughts and actions are shaped by various sources of emotional pollution.

Sources of Emotional Pollution

Emotional pollution is present in all cultures. The term *culture* represents the totality of experiences and beliefs present at a particular point in time. These ideas provide the framework for individuals to gain a sense of safety and safety while trying to make sense of the world around them. In spite of the many positive aspects of these organizational structures, emotional pollution naturally results. The most obvious way is how individuals make assumptions about certain types of people, places and things. It is difficult if not impossible to change these ideas and the type and amount of emotional pollution associated with them. The reason why is related to how children learn certain patterns of behavior in order to be accepted by parents, siblings, friends and teachers; and later, spouses, employers and society in general. Another highly emotional issue arises when a tradition is questioned. Many adults seem to feel they are rejecting their parents or disrespecting previous generations when they do so. This type of thinking is the reason why individuals often emit pollutants when discussing certain topics.

Places of worship create emotional pollution. Most religions reflect a narrow view of what is appropriate and inappropriate behavior. Those who vary from the accepted norms are perceived as in need of spiritual help. This common perspective coupled with a general lack of sensitivity, often results in emotional pollution. An example occurs when people are led to believe if they help others, they will be perceived favorably by a higher power. Granted, that may be true, yet, no evidence exists to verify it. Religious-based emotional pollutants also surface as justifications for certain types of behavior. An example is a corporate leader who emphasizes productivity to the detriment of workers. She continually requires employees to become more productive while providing low wages and limited benefits. Then, as the corporation becomes more prosperous, she defends her actions by making statements such as, "I am helping people by creating jobs;" "With the money I earn, I donate to all these worthy causes including a large proportion to my church." In spite of these types of comments, religion is frequently used to justify policies and procedures resulting in emotional pollution.

Schools are another source of emotional pollution. In traditional classrooms, children are relatively passive in the learning process as the teacher does most of the talking while students spend their time at their desks listening, responding when called upon, and completing assigned tasks (Skinner & Belmont, 1993). Student progress is usually determined by how well they perform on a uniform set of standards for their grade. This emphasis on definitive answers does not lend itself to critical thinking or the notion of a range of answers. Rather, a one-size fits all perspective results in large amounts of emotional pollution. In contrast, in an open classroom, teachers assume a flexible authority role sharing decision-making with children. Curriculum experiences not only include basic information, but also structured activities promoting and nurturing imagination, creativity and problem-solving skills. In this approach, student performance is evaluated in relation to their prior development. In spite of the many benefits of an open classroom, federal and state education policy-makers continue to stress the importance of objective information. This mindset typically leads to an overemphasis on cognitive skills rather than the development of the whole child. With that being the norm, limited learning opportunities are designed to help students acquire emotional literacy skills.

Student discipline policies influence the amount of emotional pollution in schools. Of course, there must be some level of control and order for students to learn. Nevertheless, most school cultures emphasize conformity to the detriment of individuality.

An example is school uniforms. Many educators, parents and community members believe this will result in improved behavior and increased learning. In some situations, that may be true, but not others. Another pollutant is the structure of student codes of conduct. In most United States school districts, a three-tiered system is used to teach appropriate behavior. This approach results in vast amounts of emotional pollution because unacceptable behavior is treated the same regardless of individual and circumstantial differences. School discipline practices are also impacted by the well-being of educators. As in any other profession, a number of teachers are not emotionally healthy. This unfortunate reality at times causes adults to act similar to children. For example, if a student emotionally violates the teacher by not following class rules, some respond by disrespecting them. Regrettably, youth are more likely to leave school early or graduate with limited abilities and skills when they frequently participate in this detrimental sequence of events.

The media also creates and shapes emotional pollution. The images and sounds of television movies, music and videogames affect how children and adults react to environmental stimuli. In many instances, this results in children and adults becoming vulnerable to particular types of emotional pollution. Examples are television commercials influencing children to ask their parents to purchase the latest video game or cell phone. Media pollutants also affect how individuals perceive themselves. Some develop a negative sense of self when they compare their life to the celebrities, athletes and corporate leaders portrayed in the media. As this ongoing aspect of the human condition unfolds, many adults ultimately adopt a personal perspective in which they determine their worth or value in comparison to others.

Many examples of this are evident every day. For instance, why do parents with limited resources purchase Nike shoes for their newborn; granted, they look nice, but why spend large amounts of money on something that does not have anything to do with keeping their child's feet warm? The logical answer is they want to be perceived favorably by those around them. Another related illustration is how some adults are willing to take financial risks to purchase a home they really cannot afford. Many seem to be convinced their life would be better if they had a place of their own. This norm-referenced life perspective reflects how the media plays a significant role in emotional pollution.

Sources of emotional pollution are families, places of worship, schools and the media. Many pollutants are associated with increasing divorce rates, remarriage and blended families. Places of worship as well discuss a number of emotion-based issues that contribute to social disharmony. Some of which include love, sin, abortion and eternal life. As one might also expect, this ongoing sense of emotional uneasiness and discomfort becomes a constant societal reality when schools do not teach emotional literacy. Rather, the focus in most United States schools is on finite skills measured on a standardized test. The media also relies on emotional pollution to shape certain thoughts and corresponding actions. Currently, a culture of fear and a sense of hopelessness guide many responses to emotional pollution.

Responses to Emotional Pollution

People instinctively try to avoid or escape the discomfort and pain associated with emotional pollution. This strategy to some degree is helpful, but in some situations, it is not. When that is the case, individuals often gain comfort by interacting with others having similar physical appearances, interests, shared experiences and perspectives. This self-preservation process begins when a young child acts like their mother, father or other care provider. As they become older and enter adolescents, they usually adopt the views of their parents while struggling to find their own sense of self. In the course of this life progression, coping strategies develop to offset emotional pollution. These actions can be described using a level of force continuum beginning with no response and ending with physical confrontations. Points in between represent word selection, degrees of voice tone, and general descriptions of attitude. An example is a two-person conversation. If one participant begins to experience discomfort, nonverbal messages communicate what is felt at that particular moment. Then, if the other person does not pick-up on the subtleties, words are used in an attempt to gain immediate comfort and a general sense of safety and security. If some form of relief however is not attained, other more direct terms are expressed with a louder voice tone. In some cases, the outcome of these actions will continue the conservation; other times, the discomfort magnifies into a level of pain ultimately ending the discussion. Another level of force illustration occurs when television commentators discuss a current event. Many struggle with the ability to let someone finish what they are saying. As they interrupt, they become louder; this often triggers other panelists to exhibit similar behavior. At the end of what is normally a brief discussion, the content of the conversation is usually forgotten and what is remembered is how people talked over each other.

A person's mood influences where they are on the level of force continuum. The more negative, the greater likelihood they are closer to physical confrontation than no response.

This reflects how emotional pollution intensifies the innate sense of fear. These uncomfortable feelings frequently cause individuals to wonder what really is the truth regarding a particular matter. Without clarity and confidence, a collective sense of insecurity creates an atmosphere where many are emotionally hypersensitive to the comments and actions of others. Individuals are more likely to exhibit increased levels of force when this happens. In some cases, emotional pollution reaches a point in which adults feel the need to "come out swinging" in order to survive in a world that is insensitive to them. Most cannot tolerate the discomfort and pain any longer; something drastic must be done. Increased voice tone, profanity, physical aggression and illegal activities often occur in response to their sense of outrage.

Children and adults respond to emotional pollution in a variety of other ways. The most obvious is how words are used to gain a sense of order. Individuals experience less discomfort when they can describe, define and categorize persons, places and things. When something however is new, unknown or unexplainable, it creates ongoing uneasiness. An example in a work environment is how employees react to a recently hired co-worker. The person is normally observed to determine if they are worthy of belonging to the existing group. If not, subtle emotion-based nonverbal and verbal messages are communicated to adapt to the existing standards or leave. Of course, these actions are a form of emotional pollution. Another organization-based illustration is how customers might react if they entered a large department store having items in no particular order. More than likely, feelings of confusion and disarray would cause them to leave. The ability to label, classify and judge things help individuals feel in greater control; thus, lessening the negative effects of emotional pollution.

People also try to distract themselves from emotional pollution. These thoughts and actions consist of a variety of things like reading fictional stories, writing poetry and music, participating or observing sports and watching television. Many of these types of activities are encouraged and reinforced through statements like, "everybody needs a hobby to lessen their stress" or "they just need to stop being so serious and have more fun in life." Adults as well are conditioned to believe vacations are a way to temporarily escape the mundane aspects of life. For some, these common coping strategies have limited positive effects. When that is the case, emotional pollution sometimes becomes so unbearable adults rely on mood altering activities and substances to cope with their ongoing difficulties. Examples include those who excessively exercise, over or under eat, and use alcohol or other drugs to deal with discomfort and pain. In spite of the many negative aspects of distractors, they are valuable. If individuals did not have them, they would be more likely to have a heightened sense of anger and would be dangerous to be around; others might be unable to sleep due to the constant internal noise created by negative thoughts. In addition, without distractors, emotional pollution would be so rampant in society it would be almost impossible to be happy. If that were the case, the world would become an even more difficult place to live.

Rationalizations are a less obvious response to emotional

pollution. They act as defense mechanisms to buffer or distort emotions. For example, when difficulties arise, people sometimes state, "It's just the way it is, and I cannot do anything about it" or "I do not have any other choice." These assertions allow individuals to continue their daily activities rather than dwelling on the discomfort associated with a particular experience. In most situations, comparisons to others provide the foundation for rationalizations. It is common for instance to hear the statement "I can't do that, what will people think" or "that's not how we do things here." In other circumstances, adults seem to feel better by evaluating their plight in life to those who are portrayed in the media as experiencing ongoing challenges. Many think but are hesitant to state, "At least I do not have to deal with what those poor people have too." Rationalizations as well help adults avoid confrontations. Statements like, "He is a good person, so I am sure he did not mean in that way" reflect the desire to escape something that might possibly create discomfort. Ongoing emotional pollution results when individuals are hesitant to communicate honestly.

To summarize, people develop a variety of coping strategies to offset the discomfort and pain associated with emotional pollution. These actions fall along a level of force continuum beginning with no response to physical confrontations. Points in between represent word selection, degrees of voice tone, and general descriptions of attitude. An individual's mood influences where they are on the continuum. The more negative, the greater likelihood emotional pollution increases the use of force. Children and adults also learn other ways to respond to emotional pollution. Words are used to gain a sense of safety and security.

Unfortunately, though, not every person, place or thing fits neatly into some predetermined category. As children and adults realize this, many develop ways to rationalize and distract themselves from the discomfort and pain they are experiencing. In spite of these and other learned patterns of behavior, increasing numbers of adults are experiencing depression, terminating marriages, committing acts of violence, are unemployed or underemployed, and in poor physical health. As these societal trends continue, most people are unaware of how their responses to emotional pollution affect the quality of life.

Chapter Summary

This chapter described a form of environmental pollution always present but rarely discussed. It is emotional pollution. Emotional pollution is the innate, environmental or combination of elements negatively affecting thoughts and actions. These toxins consist of a variety of interconnected variables. From a biological point of view, an individual's autonomic nervous system determines the frequency and extent of emotional pollution. Survival-based perceptions of environmental stimuli govern this process. From a cultural perspective, feelings of discomfort and pain trigger the creation and emission of emotional pollution. This normally occurs within the context of communication, morality, and a host of other situation-specific experiences. As this multifaceted dynamic unfolds, an emotional pollution cycle develops in which individuals and groups exhibit actions to help them feel better while simultaneously creating difficulties for others. Those affected then demonstrate similar actions. This characteristic of the human experience is the reason why people struggle to identify the beauty around them or when they do, it is only for a brief moment. Instead, most are fearful, worrying how they will survive in a world perceived as insensitive to them.

Families, places of worship, schools and the media were presented as sources of emotional pollution. Many pollutants are linked to increasing divorce rates, remarriages, and blended families. Similarly, places of worship discuss a variety of emotion-based issues that at times create disharmony among societal members. This ongoing sense of public tension often lingers and intensifies when educators do not teach emotional literacy. Rather, the focus in most United States schools is on finite skills measured on a standardized test. The media also relies on emotional pollution to shape certain thoughts and actions. Currently, it promotes a culture of fear and a sense of hopelessness among many. These emotions and corresponding thoughts often trigger a general sense of uneasiness.

The chapter ends with a discussion of responses to emotional pollution. These coping strategies fall along a level of force continuum beginning with no action to physical confrontations. In between these extremes are behaviors reflecting a person's mood. In most instances, the more negative someone is the greater likelihood they depend on words to label and categorize persons, places and things. However, as children and adults realize that not everything fits neatly into some predetermined box; their sense of discomfort often leads to the emission of emotional pollution. As this pattern of behavior unfolds, rationalizations and distractors are commonly used to justify and escape the negative effects of emotional pollution. People also usually become more aggressive if these coping strategies provide limited relief and comfort. This typically results in many individual and societal outcomes. Chapter Two discusses some of them.

Chapter 2
Emotional Pollution Outcomes

Emotional pollution is the innate, environmental or combination of elements negatively affecting thoughts and actions. This always present but rarely discussed environmental pollutant is produced and emitted when individuals feel discomfort and pain. The autonomic nervous system plays a role in this process. It is comprised of two subsystems: sympathetic and parasympathetic (Siegel, 2010). In the sympathetic system, large amounts of energy are expended in response to survival-based environmental stimuli. As feelings of 'fight, flight or freeze" are encountered, increased adrenalin, heart rate and level of arousal result in vast amounts of emotional pollution. However, once obtaining a sense of personal safety, individuals gradually transition into their own unique state of physical and psychological balance in the parasympathetic system. When that occurs, emotional pollution lessens in frequency and intensity while becoming more abstract. Children and adults today, just like in the past, emit emotional pollution in order to feel better at a particular moment. Those affected then exhibit similar type behaviors. This ongoing cycle of emotional pollution leads to a variety of individual and societal outcomes. Some of which will be discussed in the upcoming chapter.

Individual Outcomes

Emotional pollution affects an individual's brain. More specifically, the frequency and intensity experienced influences the way in which memory, language and motor functions develop. For some, emotional pollution results in certain parts of the brain being underdeveloped. When that is the case, basic survival instincts are more likely to dominate responses to environmental stimuli. Adults with this characteristic may also be predisposed to experience fewer positive emotions. For instance, feelings of joy related to the birth of a new family member or the laughter of a comedian may not enter consciousness; or, if it does, it is not as often or intense as others experience. Ongoing emotional pollution also effects the sleep-wake cycle. Discomfort and pain lead to ongoing tossing and turning in bed, and limited rest; others, at times respond by sleeping too much. Whatever the case might be, emotional pollution makes it difficult to obtain an intricate balance between rest and movement. A number of interconnected outcomes happen because of this. A person's body is more likely to hurt without appropriate rest. This increases the chance someone participates in the emotional pollution cycle. Deficits in sleep as well increase the frequency and intensity of fear, shame and guilt. These uncomfortable feelings sometimes lead to responses labeled as irritability, mad, insensitive and hyperactive. Historically, these types of actions have played a negative role in personal freedom, quality of life, racism, poverty, immigration, justice and public health.

Emotional pollution influences a person's mood. Moods are emotional states representing how an individual perceives themselves, others, and the events occurring around them. Those who are optimistic are more likely to generate and project positive energy. They too are more apt to think with greater clarity and efficiency to solve complex problems. In contrast, adults with a negative mood often view the world as ugly, demeaning and scary. These perspectives adversely affect judgment and sometimes result in negative lifestyle choices. Emotional pollution increases the amount of time with a negative mood. This is normally reflected in the level of stress someone creates for him or herself. Examples are parents who feel there are not enough hours in the day to complete all the things that need doing. As this way of thinking develops, emotional pollution not only influences perspective but also contributes to high blood pressure, diabetes and other chronic ailments. Adults with these difficult medical conditions appear trapped in an emotional state in which they believe they have little control over their body. This helpless feeling plays a significant role in shaping their personality.

Freud (1938) suggested the id, ego, and superego comprise personality. The ego balances the natural pleasure-seeking tendency (the id) of individuals and their conscience (the superego). Emotional pollution to some degree attacks ego. When that occurs, individuals use a variety of coping strategies to obtain a sense of safety and security. However, if limited comfort is attained, anger usually arises and leads to actions labeled as pettiness, sarcasm, spite, resentment and hatefulness. These types of behavior promote division rather than closeness among people. For many, this also teaches them how to communicate in ways to avoid discomfort and pain. In most conversations, neutral or emotionally limited words are used to discuss some broad issue like the weather or sports. These surface conversations continue until the topic is exhausted or someone becomes uncomfortable with what has been said. At that point, emotional pollution is emitted to alter the discussion. If these subtle nonverbal movements or changes in voice tone are not successful, a more direct action is taken. The most obvious is one person walking away from the other. By doing so, their immediate need to escape the uncomfortable situation is met; the other participant though may feel disrespected, as what was discussed is often devalued and forgotten.

A number of outcomes occur because of emotional pollutions effect on personality. The most significant is a loss of trust in others. Adults often become guarded, cautious and hesitant in response to discomfort and pain. This sometimes results in them withdrawing from normal activities or only associating with those who have similar beliefs, experiences and perspectives. An increased need for belonging is another common occurrence. To fit in, many if not all individuals develop an emotion-based mask to cover-up or filter emotions. Many challenges arise when this happens. An example is the ability to work with others. Granted, some desired task is completed; nevertheless, it may only represent an outcome partially reflecting the true abilities of those involved. Another difficulty is some people may lose sight of their true identity. The mask becomes who they are rather than a temporary way to offset discomfort and pain. Adults also seem to learn how to adjust their mask based on the demands of the environment. For instance, in an employment situation the mask is usually securely fastened in order to be perceived favorably. In contrast, with a group of friends, the mask might be loosely attached or not present. Regardless of how tight the mask might be, just having one reflects how emotional pollution affects a person's life.

The discomfort and pain associated with emotional pollution

increases the need for acceptance. Examples of this occur in many different situations. For instance, some friends are meeting at a local restaurant for dinner. Frank decides to order a steak, potato, salad and a gourmet dessert. The waiter arrives a few minutes later with a hot dog, French fries, and a brownie wrapped in plastic. Frank quickly realizes he did not order the items; nevertheless, he eats them thinking it is the socially appropriate thing to do. As the evening progresses, everyone seems to be having a good time. The waiter then arrives with the bill. Frank is charged for what he ordered. He proceeds to pay for the items despite not receiving them. Why would Frank do such a thing? He is not wealthy. Franks' need to be perceived favorably and desire to be a part of the group may explain his actions. Another example sometimes happens in an employment setting. Many adults are thankful to have a job even though they complain about a lack of leadership, working conditions and long hours. When talking to them, many eventually state, "I like my employer." How can they say that when a few minutes earlier they grumbled about the many negative aspects of their job? Emotional pollution is the reason why some would convince themselves they are not devalued. Their need for money to pay bills also distorts the reality in which they are living. Once payday arrives however, their limited purchasing power results in high levels of discomfort, pain and anger. These feelings along with the ongoing need for acceptance cause many adults to spend an inordinate amount time thinking about their job. This overemphasis on work contributes to a variety of other emotional pollution outcomes.

Emotional pollution makes it difficult to determine the truth. The more frequent and intense someone experiences pollutants, the greater likelihood discomfort and pain skews their perspective. As this occurs, individuals rely on words to make sense of the world around them. For example, Leo Canner invented the term *autism* to label children and adolescents who are withdrawn and have limited language ability (Turnbull, Turnbull, Wehmeyer & Shogren, 2020). Parents having children with these types of behavior seem to feel better simply knowing what to call the condition. The need for order is also represented by hierarchal structures. These configurations act as natural buffers to offset the uncertainty associated with the unknown. In most cases, those at the top or in positions of power ultimately determine what is considered true. Organizations also appear to become more rigid when emotional pollution creates or adds to the ambiguity associated with some policy or procedure. An obvious example is the military; if orders and the chain of command are not followed, someone might die. The medical professions intervention protocols are similar.

The need for order causes some individuals to feel rejected. Those who experience this often conform to some arbitrary societal standard in order to avoid discomfort and pain. This pattern of behavior is a form of self-oppression. For example, adults who adopt the characteristics of others willing relinquish part of their identity. By doing so, they disenfranchise themselves by losing some degree of control over the events occurring in their life. Granted, no one can be an island onto him or herself; many though feel "boxed in" because of their membership in a particular group. An example is how most if not all employees perform tasks they are uncomfortable with in order to maintain their job. Statements such as, "I need the money and health insurance, so that's why I am doing what I am doing" make this point quite evident. Regardless of how people rationalize their actions, emotionally, many are bothered and at times upset by what they must do in order to be part of something larger then themselves.

Lastly, emotional pollution hinders personal growth. This normally goes unnoticed because an individual's sense of self develops within a culture promoting sameness rather than difference. An example of this occurred when a college-student was asked; does it bother you your children will not be exposed to various art forms or participate in physical education programs in the public schools? After pausing for a few seconds, the mom said, "I did not have it either, and I turned out ok." Other comments like "I can agree with that" reflect how the discomfort and pain associated with emotional pollution limits the amount of information thought about. From a broader perspective, hiring practices often stymie imagination, creativity and innovation. Employers often use the phrase "a good fit" to indicate how it is more important to them someone can work with the current staff rather than having new ideas.

Summary of Emotional Pollution and Individual Outcomes

Emotional pollution results in a variety of interrelated outcomes. The most significant is how the structure and abilities of parts of the brain are impacted. Logically, the frequency and intensity of emotional pollution experienced determines its effect on memory, language and motor skills. These abilities as well are impacted by the sleep-wake cycle. The greater the difficulty obtaining rest, the more likely someone's personality develops and is present within the context of a negative mood. A number of complex issues arise when a pessimistic attitude dominates thoughts. Trust is one. When adults are hesitant and at times scared to trust others, they often wear an invisible "mask" to cover-up their true feelings. This self-preservation strategy helps them obtain a sense of safety and security while at the same time creating an atmosphere of confusion between and among people. As this occurs, an increased need for belonging, acceptance and order limits personal growth. The extent and degree in which this occurs determines the level in which emotional pollution affects an individual's identity and general quality of life. It too brings to light how emotional pollutions impact on individuals leads to a variety of societal outcomes.

Emotional Pollution and Societal Outcomes

A number of societal outcomes result because of emotional pollution. Some of which will be discussed in the following pages. The reader is reminded that the information presented is based on personal observations and not scientific studies. Nevertheless, awareness of emotional pollution may help lessen some of the difficulties occurring in the world today. Please also note the word *outcome* rather than *problem* is purposefully used. An outcome is something measurable whereas a problem is a value judgment based on interpretation of data. With these caveats in mind, it is now time to explore how emotional pollution contributes to societal outcomes. To begin, personal relationships are discussed.

Emotional pollution is linked to human survival instincts. The greater the frequency and extent encountered; the more likely individuals emit pollutants to protect themselves. As this occurs, personal relationships are limited or strained. When that is the case, some are prone to struggle meeting their most basic needs. In extreme situations, a lack of food and shelter might cause others to feel devalued and perhaps even invisible (See Ellison, 1952). These types of thoughts often create an internal narrative in which someone perceives themselves as not worthy of love and compassion. This distorted self-perception hinders the amount and quality of personal relationships. It too creates an environment where most actions to some degree reflect a survival mentality. An example is the widely held "push through" or "grind it out" attitude. Even when tired, many adults think they should keep going rather than rest. If they do stop, some worry about being perceived as lazy. The statement "I'm ok" is another conditioned response affecting relationships. It reflects how children and adults judge what they are experiencing rather than allowing things to unfold naturally. Of course, judgments are a part of life. However, they often lead to actions hindering the development of friendships. Another sometimes-detrimental way of thinking is to try to "make things better." This desire often creates an atmosphere of ongoing uneasiness as individuals search for something impossible to find. It too increases the likelihood someone is critical of others. Statements like "they have become complacent" or "there in it for the wrong reasons" divide rather than unite people.

Survival and Caring

A culture of caring is limited by the extent in which emotional pollution creates a survival mentality. Survival, in this context, not only consists of food and shelter but also the ability to maintain a desired lifestyle. In most instances, adults become more self-centered when their basic needs or way of life is threatened. As this instinct-based pattern of behavior unfolds, a person's sense of safety determines their potential for caring. Caring is a loving feeling that exhibits concern and empathy for others (Merriam-Webster Online Dictionary, 2009). It usually happens when two or more individuals come together in such a way an opportunity for human compassion exists. These types of actions can be plotted along a continuum beginning with self-centeredness, unaware of those around you, and ending with the loss of life protecting someone. In between these extremes, contextual and situational variables determine acts of caring. At the most basic level, children learn to interact with others by observing adults. Usually, if their parents demonstrate caring, they are more likely to exhibit similar behavior. As they become older, neighborhood and school experiences then either reinforce or negate their previously held beliefs. For example, if a student has a series of compassionate teachers, they are more likely to learn how certain thoughts and actions affect the lives of others. Yet, in spite of these positive models, emotional pollution continues to play a significant role in a global culture of caring.

Emotional pollution hinders the development of skills needed for caring. Listening is one such ability. When individuals encounter pollutants, discomfort and pain usually distract them from what is being said. They too normally struggle to gain information when their level of uneasiness does not tolerate delay, provocation or annoyance. Another issue is how individuals vary in their interpretation of information. These differences in perception of voice tone, pitch, rate, color, texture and nonverbal messages make it difficult to understand the perspectives of others. Without knowing, acts of caring are less likely to occur and if they do, many are well intentioned but misguided. Emotional pollution also affects memory. In most instances, basic survival instincts cause children and adults to remember negative rather than positive experiences. For example, if someone feels harmed in some way by their parents, friends, teachers or employers, they are more likely to recall the exact events. In contrast, if something pleasant happened at the grocery store, it is often forgotten. Acts of caring are less apt to take place when negative experiences are remembered more than positive.

The dynamics of a typical conversation further illustrate the role of emotional pollution in caring. A discussion consists of two or a group of individuals voluntarily engaged. Initially, a thought is stated verbally; others, then respond or convey subtle nonverbal cues that they are not interested in the subject. If the conversation though continues, individuals gradually become less capable of hearing and listening. In extreme cases, uneasiness may adversely affect relationships. Conversations as well are shaped by how pollutants affect emotional intimacy. If a high level of closeness exists, the discussion has a greater likelihood of continuing; if not, participants seem guarded, afraid to hurt the feelings of others. An adult's emotional reaction to topics like politics and religion also sometimes hinders the ability to listen. When that is the case, acts of caring are often associated with issues briefly entering consciousness. A common example is donating money for a particular cause. Children and adults' benefit, nevertheless, they usually are emotionally disconnected with those providing assistance.

A sense of marginalization arises when a limited culture of caring exists. Statements such as, "No one is looking out for me, or no one cares what happens to me," reflect how some individuals and groups perceive themselves as unimportant. Those with this mindset are more prone to experience feelings of insecurity, despair, hopelessness and helplessness. In response, their actions usually range from trying to escape whatever is causing discomfort or pain to physical aggression. In between these extremes, are behaviors shaped by the type and amount of emotional pollution experienced. An example occurs when driving an automobile. When someone is perceived as endangering another, the other person usually honks his or her horn to express anger. By doing so, they send the message "Hey, what are you doing;" "Pay attention and stop talking on the phone when you are driving." As the other driver hears the sound, they often wonder, "Are they honking at me, or what's their problem." In extreme situations, some form of road rage happens. When thinking more about life experiences and caring, it is clear that most actions are self-centered rather than altruistic. This is the reason why many individuals and groups feel slighted and harmed regardless of the situation or circumstances surrounding their experiences. Words such as, *unfairness, discrimination, injustice, disenfranchised* and *inequality* illuminate this perspective.

People often depend on others for help when feeling

marginalized. For instance, in the United States, many citizens believe the federal, state or local government is responsible to solve their problems. Still, regardless of what legislation is passed; some individual or group thinks they are being mistreated. An example is the number of adults who believe they are unfairly targeted by law enforcement because of their color or ethnic origin. Protest marches and confrontations with police usually result. In response, state and local officials try to deescalate the situation by holding news conferences, removing current leaders and establishing advisory committees to identify ways to solve problems. These actions normally calm things down temporarily; long-term change though usually does not happen. As people, realize this, an ongoing sense of a lack of caring leads to acts of aggression. This normally happens when individuals have reached a point in which they feel the need to "come out swinging" in order to survive in a world insensitive to them. They cannot tolerate being disrespected any longer; something drastic must be done. Another related observation is how easily led individuals are when someone provides a sense of caring. For example, if a young adult is consistently hungry and sleeping in a cardboard box, anyone who gives them hope will usually be followed. This is the reason why some are willing to fight and die in the name of certain guiding principles or religious beliefs. Extreme hatred and killing is the ultimate negative outcome of emotional pollutions impact on a global culture of caring.

A culture of caring exists to the degree in which emotional pollution leads to a survival mentality. If the majority of people are in a state of trying to protect themselves, limited acts of caring occur. When this happens, some individuals and groups naturally feel marginalized. Their discomfort and pain then usually cause them to do certain things to feel better. While doing so, they create difficulties for others. The emotional pollution cycle continues as always. Emotional pollution also impedes the development of skills needed for caring. The ability to listen and understand others is difficult when the innate, environmental or combination of elements comprising emotional pollution are present. Many adults respond by becoming more self-centered. As this characteristic of the human condition unfolds, complex issues related to human dignity, kindness, compassion and equality create an ongoing struggle between individuals and groups. These challenges reflect how emotional pollution affects caring.

Emotional Pollution and Fear

The collective accumulation of emotional pollution creates a culture of fear. These feelings have the broad capability to alter every aspect of existence, from life expectancy to gross domestic product. More specifically, when adults spend a large amount of time being afraid, they are more likely to consume substances detrimental to their health, withdraw from people who care about them and purchase items they cannot afford. When that is the case, some experience a level of discomfort and pain that parallels a physical fight perceived as never ending and impossible to win. This state of being begins to develop when parents model actions that communicate to their children how the world is out to harm them and they should be on guard to protect themselves. Recent school shootings perpetuate this mindset. For instance, state and local education leaders have allocated resources to upgrade buildings to make it more difficult to enter. They too have hired additional armed school resource officers. This, along with the ongoing emphasis on standardized achievement test results creates a learning environment where a number of students struggle with fear and anxiety. These uncomfortable feelings play a significant role in the frequency and extent children and adolescents emit emotional pollution as adults.

The more fearful someone is, the greater the likelihood they emit emotional pollution. This usually occurs within the context of trying to gain some level of control. Often, this is a part of an individual's vocational identity. An example is an employee who feels their job is the only place where they have the power to influence what they experience. In some situations, though, they are unaware of how others perceive them as rude and disrespectful because they constantly try to protect their company position and false sense of authority. What is also common is how they respond when a customer requests to speak to their supervisor; in many instances, their actions reflect instinctive responses such as, raising their voice and blaming someone else or a company policy for their behavior. From a broader point of view, it is difficult to be sensitive to the needs of others when searching for some level of control and power. This is the reason why world leaders continue to struggle with geopolitical issues related to human rights, economies, climate change and health care systems.

A culture of fear leads to conformity. This normally results in the acceptance and continuation of many indoctrinated beliefs. An example is the education level required for certain professions. For instance, teachers normally have four years of formal education before they can instruct children; a lawyer has six prior to practicing law, and medical doctors have at least eight before independently treating a patient. Who has created these arbitrary guidelines? Some people surely have the innate ability to become a teacher, lawyer or doctor without all the required years of training. Another related observation is the clothes worn in different occupations. Suits and ties are expected of lawyers, doctors have white coats, and educators wear casual attire. These and other conformity-based ideas provide a sense of collective order. However, they also promote dependency on others. Instead of having a sense of empowerment, many adults feel someone other than them will determine their plight in life. This mindset is captured in the concept of social capital. Whom you know rather than your abilities determine opportunities in life. Why try so hard to gain something when others seem to attain it with little or no effort? "Life is not fair" is the comment usually used to explain this everyday reality. This type of rationalization acts as an ongoing catalyst for instinctive and conditioned responses to fear.

The most common reaction to fear is to move physically away from whatever is causing it. In other situations, if acute or persistent periods are present, certain people, environments and experiences are avoided. Adults as well develop psychological boundaries or walls to protect themselves from these difficult feelings. Still, when barriers are challenged, ongoing uneasiness causes them to try to escape the situation. This sometimes happens after someone has recently been divorced. In social situations, regardless of physical attraction, the person nonverbally or verbally communicates they are not ready to be emotionally vulnerable again. In some instances, it may take months or even years to process their past feelings. When they are ready, it may require large amounts of time to develop a close relationship. These and other similar types of self-preservation actions limit the number of individuals someone will interact with during their lifetime. This may result in lost opportunities to learn and enjoy the company of others. An airport terminal provides a setting to think further about this. While waiting for a connecting flight, hundreds of people walk by that you have never seen before. Some of them probably would be fun to be around and share a variety of experiences. Unfortunately, though, the fear associated with emotional pollution causes most adults to interact with others much like them. A person's quality of life is affected when this happens.

Another common fear-based response is to compare your life to others. For example, the graphic images of violence in Syria or starvation in Ethiopia distract attention from the realities of one's own situation. Just having knowledge of the experiences of the less fortunate often helps to feel better. Statements such as, "My life is not that bad; look at those poor folks," and "Do you see how they are living?" make this point evident. Similar types of comments occur when adults are afraid to do something. Many verbalize, "I can't do that; what will people think of me" or "It's just the way it is, and nothing can be done about it." These verbalizations act as defense mechanisms to avoid uncomfortable feelings. A number of issues arise when this coping strategy is used. The most significant is to deny your own humanity. Without accepting emotions as they are, a part of identity is lost. This increases the likelihood emotional pollution will play a significant role in life. In addition, letting go of past negative experiences is almost impossible when not emotionally honest. Instead, struggles with self-esteem increase in frequency and intensity. To offset this, labeling and judging persons, places and things usually happens. This strategy helps individuals gain comfort while at the same time it often promotes division rather than closeness between and among people. From a broad perspective, this lack of self-awareness and sensitivity to the needs of others is the reason why emotional pollution continues to lead to decisions negatively affecting people, animals and the environment.

Routines are a less obvious way to cope with fear. These sequences of events provide a level of safety and security needed to participate in daily activities. In most cases, an individual's physical and psychological health determines the extent in which these arbitrary patterns of behavior are relied upon. For instance, the younger or older a person is the more benefit they gain from highly structured environments. Teachers and long-term health care providers capitalize on this as they design learning opportunities and independent living activities. A consistent sleep-wake cycle and diet also helps to cope with life's challenges. In some instances, however, rigid schedules limit opportunities to develop and nurture imagination, creativity and problem-solving abilities. Innate talent is more likely to go unnoticed when this happens. Another issue is how people react when emotional pollution causes them to deviate from their routines. For some, a crisis arises. An example is someone who purchases groceries on Wednesday. Even when sick, they have to do so. Not accomplishing their "to do" list causes them to feel even worse. Those having these types of thoughts are more than likely limited by a perspective shaped and governed by fear. As always, the fear associated with emotional pollution will continue to result in collective decisions benefitting some to the detriment of others. This is the reason why broad societal changes rarely if ever happen.

Emotional pollution adds to the innate fear associated with survival. Most human actions to some degree are therefore attempts to gain a sense of safety and security. This of course is difficult to recognize because it is more psychological rather than physical. An example occurs when an individual is asked a question that makes them uncomfortable. She impulsively reacts by verbally responding without much thought. What is said is incorrect; and, it is perceived as a lie. This lessens her creditability and respect from others. Once she realizes this, a group identity is often sought to gain a sense of acceptance. While doing so, she voluntarily relinquishes a part of her identity. Collectively, this common pattern of behavior results in a variety of societal issues. Some of which are present within the context of a norm-referenced cultural perspective.

Norm-Referenced Perspective

Emotional pollution increases the basic human need for acceptance. This has led to a norm-referenced cultural perspective in which individuals compare their life to others. In most instances, some arbitrary criteria are used to determine personal worth and value. Historically in the United States, the American Dream of a home, two-car garage and white picket fence was a measure of success. Today, outward appearances of money continue to influence decisions. For instance, some young adults with limited resources purchase new automobiles.

Granted, it probably makes them feel good. Why though would they want to have a large monthly payment when struggling to have enough food to eat? The logical answer is they want to be perceived favorably. Another related example is how some are willing to take huge financial risks to purchase a home they really cannot afford. Many seem convinced that life would be better if they had a place of their own. This norm-referenced life perspective is also present in governmental policies affecting world events. For example, the multifaceted interconnecting issues related to free trade agreements, oil prices and human rights highlight how leaders are frequently in a state of comparison.

A norm-referenced perspective has always been a part of the human condition. However, it has become more apparent recently due to a number of variables. The most obvious is the quality of life in industrialized countries has reached a point where most people have basic subsistence. As the standard of living has increased, adults have more time and energy to spend on tasks other than providing food and shelter for their family. In spite of these significant lifestyle changes, emotional pollution continues to trigger an innate hunter and gatherer mentality. Today, financial portfolios, vacation homes and other material possessions have replaced the search for water and game (deer, turkey, etc.). Another outcome of a higher standard of living is that many people have not experienced a lack of something. As a result, some struggle determining the difference between what they need and want. This point is evident when considering the number of individuals feeling entitled to an automobile, computer, cell phone and designer clothing. An additional related issue is parents who want to make their child's life better than their own. Despite positive intentions, "helicopter" and "snowplow" parenting styles hinder the development of skills needed to participate in daily activities. From a broad perspective, this affects the workforce. Some employers struggle to locate and hire adults having basic job-related skills like being on time, dressing appropriately and working consistently. These deficits in "soft skills" not only play in role in the economy but also contribute to the ongoing creation and emission of emotional pollution.

The media promotes the link between acceptance and a norm-referenced life perspective. For example, why do some parents with limited money purchase expensive Nike baby shoes? Obviously, their infant is unaware of the significance of the logo; nevertheless, advertisements promoting their status influence the purchase of them. Network television characters and story lines also convey what personal success is. Usually, it is a certain body image, location of residence (zip code), size of home, and type of automobile driven. In addition, the advent of twenty-four-hour news stations has increased the media's role in shaping individual and collective perspectives. For instance, when information is repeated a certain number of times, it is often believed to be true when in actuality it may not accurately reflect a diversity of viewpoints. Often, these messages are myths and misinformation such as associating happiness with a particular way of life. Adults who rely on the media to guide their thinking are more likely to adopt a lifestyle reflecting a norm-referenced perspective. They too are more vulnerable to emotional pollution as they try to obtain a sense of acceptance from others.

A norm-referenced perspective leads to a number of societal

outcomes. The most significant is how adults react when they are unable to obtain something they desperately seek. Many develop a negative attitude towards themselves and others. This sometimes results in a sense of failure, jealousy, self-pity and depression. As these feelings increase in frequency and sometimes intensify to anger and anxiety, issues related to respect arise. An example occurs in a vocational setting when an employer is oblivious to the needs of an employee. For a while, the worker is able to overlook the boss' actions; nevertheless, negative feelings accumulate. Then, at some point, insensitivity evolves into feelings of disrespect. When that occurs, individuals develop and rely upon a variety of coping mechanisms to overcome their uncomfortable feelings. An example is noticed when college graduates obtain their first "real" job. Fear, worry and vulnerability cause some to gravitate toward those physically similar to their mother, father or close friend. In other instances, their need for acceptance results in behavior they would not normally exhibit. Two common examples are conforming to some standard without thinking about it, and impulsively judging the actions of others. A norm-referenced perspective also affects the environment. Large amounts of natural resources are consumed when material possessions are associated with feelings of acceptance. An endless cycle of designing, manufacturing and transporting goods leads to environmental degradation. On a local community level, consumption is reflected in the number of trees cut down to build businesses and property storage units, amount of fuel purchased to travel to yard sales and flea markets, and water used to maintain grass and flowers. In addition, ecosystems are permanently altered when federal, state and local government policies allow individuals to build homes in areas previously preserved for plants and animals.

A number of other things happen when individuals compare themselves to others. One is emotion rather than intellect dominates thoughts. This is the reason why most actions reflect the need for immediate gratification. For example, in the United States, many citizens willingly pay large amounts of money for a few hours of entertainment rather than supporting tax increases for improvements in public safety and education. Emotion-based ideas as well explain why "gut reactions" rather than scientific studies influence how public policies are developed and implemented. With that being the norm, those in positions of power determine what is true regarding a particular matter. However, at the individual level, the truth is information supporting an emotion-based internal narrative. For instance, if someone has overcome difficulties in life they often believe others can. Those who are unable to do so are often labeled as "not trying hard enough or they simply are lazy." Another emotion-based consequence of a norm-referenced perspective is a lack of contentment. These feelings cause many adults to live within a "whirlwind" searching for something to make them happy. While doing so, ongoing emotional pollution makes it difficult to determine what the right thing to do is. Rather, most actions are self-serving, easily rationalized as appropriate. A sense of competition also arises when individuals and groups determine their status based on others. Regardless of the situation, someone has to be the winner or loser. As a result, an, us vs them mentality increases the likelihood certain life experiences trigger innate tendencies to create, emit and respond to emotional pollution. Collectively, this is the reason why social disharmony continues in spite of the many public and private actions to overcome it.

Individuals normally struggle when they do not adopt a norm-referenced perspective. In most instances, the emotional pollution associated with being different leads to feelings of confusion and an ongoing mood of sadness. When that is the case, adults have limited ability to think beyond their own needs. An example occurred when Joe was in the hospital having neck surgery. Ben, a friend, who had knowledge of the procedure did not visit him and had little contact when he returned home. Despite his previous lack of concern, Ben expected Joe's help after a minor medical procedure. Ben is perhaps not selfish, but rather his discomfort and pain may cause him to have limited insight on how his actions affect those around him. Ben also may be more likely to experience feelings of loneliness because of his lack of self-awareness and sensitivity towards others. Another way to think about acceptance is an individual's level of respect tolerance. The more tolerant to disrespect the greater likelihood emotional pollution has convinced someone they are unworthy and undeserving of high levels of compassion, respect and love. These negative self-thoughts often make it difficult to participate successfully in the activities of daily living. When that is the case, adults often rely on the medical profession to diagnose their problems and prescribe medication to help them. A number of physical and psychological issues usually arise when this happens. Those with a different perspective on life also spend an inordinate amount of time searching for others like them. When adults identify with a certain individual or group, they seem to feel better. It is as if their identity is validated because others around them have similar beliefs and perspectives. This self-insulation preservation process begins when a young child demonstrates behavior like their mother, father or other care provider. As teenagers, they typically adopt similar views as their parents while struggling to find their own particular sense of self. In the course of this complex life progression, large amounts of energy are expended developing a variety of coping strategies to offset the difficult feelings associated with being different. This use of human capital could be better spent on something else like studying and conducting research to find the cure for cancer, creating various art forms that bring joy to people or exploring the beauty of nature. The quality of human life would increase if people were more accepting of differences.

The innate need to feel accepted and liked is the reason why individuals and groups determine their worth and value in comparison to others. Emotional pollution plays a significant role in determining the extent in which this norm-referenced perspective is present within the culture. For most, the amount of emotional pollution experienced determines the degree in which they worry about what others think of them. This naturally results in patterns of behavior that are not only detrimental to children and adults but society in general. Examples include not honestly communicating with someone because you do not want to hurt their feelings. Becoming emotionally guarded to avoid a sense of personal closeness. Lastly, and perhaps most importantly, relinquishing a part of identity in order to be a part of a group. Collectively, these actions lead to a lack of trust, limited close personal relationships, and the denial and oppression of one's humanity and intellectual curiosity.

Summary of Emotional Pollution and Societal Outcomes

Emotional pollution results in a number of societal outcomes. The most obvious is how discomfort and pain acts as a barrier to personal relationships. As these uncomfortable feelings arise, linger and sometimes intensify, adults often misinterpret what others have said or written. This often leads to pollutants hindering friendships. Emotional pollution as well creates a society in which a number of individuals feel they are not worthy of love and compassion. With that being the case, a culture of caring exists only to the collective level of personal safety. Caring is a loving feeling that exhibits concern and empathy for others. It usually happens when two or more individuals come together in such a way an opportunity for human compassion exists. Many skills are required for caring to occur. The most important is the ability to listen. When someone experiences pollutants, they usually are distracted. They too normally struggle to gain information when their level of patience does not tolerate delay, provocation or annoyance. This lack of understanding is the reason why emotional pollution continues to play a significant role in many of the societal issues related to human dignity, kindness, compassion and equality.

Emotional pollution creates a culture of fear. These feelings alter every aspect of existence, from life expectancy to gross domestic product. More specifically, when adults spend a large amount of time being afraid, they often struggle to feel accepted. When that is the case, many compare their life to others. This norm-referenced point of view leads to a number of societal outcomes. One is how emotion rather than intellect dominates thoughts. This is the reason why most actions reflect the need for immediate gratification. Emotion-based thoughts as well explain why "gut reactions" rather than scientific studies guide the development of public policies. Another consequence of a norm-referenced perspective is a lack of contentment. These feelings create an atmosphere or perhaps even a sub-culture in which adults live within a "whirlwind" searching for something to make them happy. While doing so, ongoing emotional pollution makes it difficult for them to determine what the right thing to do is. Instead, most actions are self-serving, easily rationalized as appropriate. A heightened sense of competition also permeates society when acceptance and status is based on comparisons to others. This often leads to envy, jealousy, and a host of other feelings contributing to the creation and emission of emotional pollution.

Chapter Summary

This chapter discussed individual and societal outcomes associated with emotional pollution. It began with the idea the human brain is impacted by emotional pollution. For some, high levels may lead to difficulties with memory, language and motor function. When that is the case, basic survival instincts are more apt to dominate responses. Adults with this characteristic may also be prone to view the world as ugly, demeaning and scary. This negative mindset and ongoing mood is the reason why individuals struggle with issues related to trust. In response, many withdraw and become socially isolated associating only with those having similar beliefs, experiences and perspectives. When adults do venture into a new situation, they often "mask" their true feelings in order to protect themselves. As a result, some lose sight of their identity, as the mask becomes who they are rather than a temporary coping mechanism. Another issue mentioned was how emotional pollution makes it difficult to determine what the truth is. The more frequent and intense pollutants are, the greater likelihood someone relies on quick and simple answers for complex problems. Emotional pollution to some degree also attacks the human ego. When that happens, individuals rely on coping strategies to gain a sense of safety and security. However, if limited comfort is felt, anxiety and anger often lead to actions labeled as pettiness, sarcasm, spite, resentment and hatefulness. These types of behavior create division rather than closeness among people.

The second part of the chapter focused on how emotional pollution results in a number of societal outcomes. The most obvious is how discomfort and pain leads to a survival mentality. Survival, in this context not only consists of food and shelter but also maintaining a desired lifestyle. In most instances, adults become more self-centered when their basic needs or way of life is threatened. As this instinct-based pattern of behavior unfolds, personal relationships are often strained as children and adults focus on their needs and not others. This lack of sensitivity affects the level of caring present in the culture. Caring is a loving feeling that exhibits concern and empathy for others. It usually happens when two or more individuals come together in such a way an opportunity for human compassion exists. Today, just like in the past, the frequency of acts of caring exist only to the level in which people feel safe. As this cultural characteristic fluctuates, complex issues related to human dignity, kindness, compassion and equality create an ongoing struggle between individuals and groups. These challenges reflect how emotional pollution affects caring.

The collective accumulation of emotional pollution creates a culture of fear. These internal sensations alter every aspect of being, from life expectancy to gross domestic product. More specifically, when adults spend a large amount of time being afraid, they often make decisions detrimental to their health. When that happens, some experience a level of discomfort and pain similar to a never ending impossible to win physical fight. This ongoing struggle increases the basic human need for acceptance. Individuals then often compare their life to others based on some arbitrary criteria for success. A number of outcomes arise from this norm-referenced perspective. One is emotion rather than intellect dominates thoughts. This is why most actions reflect the need for immediate gratification. Emotion-based ideas as well explain why "gut reactions" rather than scientific studies influence most collective actions. Another societal consequence of a norm-referenced perspective is a lack of contentment. These feelings cause many adults to live within a "whirlwind" searching for something to make them happy. However, once they realize it is impossible to find, many exhibit patterns of behavior reflecting a lack of trust, a desire to avoid close personal relationships, and a willingness to relinquish a part of their identity to be a part of a group. A sense of competition as well permeates society when acceptance and status is based on comparisons to others. Feelings of envy, jealousy, and a host of other negative emotions usually result. A norm-referenced perspective also affects the environment.

Large amounts of natural resources are consumed when material possessions are associated with feelings of acceptance. An endless cycle of designing, manufacturing and transporting goods leads to environmental degradation and the permanent altering of plant and animal ecosystems.

Emotional pollution has been present since the existence of human beings. It is a constant much like air, wind and the ocean tides. Emotional pollution makes it virtually impossible to live in the moment. Instead, people seem to remember the discomfort and pain associated with past experiences while being anxious about the future. With that being the case, most if not all human actions are attempts to avoid or escape negative internal sensations. Individuals however are reluctant to admit that how they feel at a particular moment determines what they do. For instance, the more negative someone is the greater chance some form of aggression is used to overcome a difficult situation. If that coping strategy does not help them feel better, their level of force usually increases. As this pattern of behavior unfolds, a sense of hopelessness makes it difficult for individuals to be sensitive to those who are different from them. This lack of awareness and understanding is the reason why many actions are detrimental not only to those directly involved, but, society in general. Lastly, emotional pollution creates a global culture in which most innate talent remains dormant or nurtured to a limited degree. Often this is reflected in the way words are created and used as a form of emotional pollution. In the upcoming chapter, this idea will be discussed.

Chapter 3
Words

Emotional pollution is the innate, environmental or combination of elements negatively affecting thoughts and actions. These toxins range from subtle nonverbal messages to physical actions. In most instances, when children and adults experience discomfort and pain they emit pollutants. By doing so, they feel better while at the same time creating difficulties for others. Those affected then usually exhibit similar types of behavior. This ongoing emotional pollution cycle reflects the basic human need for self-preservation. From a literal interpretation, self-preservation is obtaining the necessary food and water to survive. However, when discussing emotional pollution, it is a relative term based on a person's life experiences. An example is how adults perceive money. For some, a distorted view exists because of the many times they have gone without something. Their thoughts and corresponding actions as a result often reflect some level of anxiety regardless of how much money they have. Other topics invoking similar types of responses are described by terms such as *fairness*, *respect*, *equality*, *discrimination* and *trust*.

An individual's perception is shaped by emotional pollution. In many situations, the energy associated with pollutants results in a negative mood. With that is the case, adults are more likely to be fearful rather than hopeful. They too often struggle with issues related to self-esteem, trust and feelings of isolation. These difficulties not only affect judgment; they also add to the level of stress someone creates for him or herself. An example is how some respond to the concept of time. Many believe there are not enough hours in the day to get everything done. This mindset promotes a state of being where words are used to offset the mental and physical challenges related to uneasiness, discomfort and pain. Words are social constructs representing a combination of sounds with an assigned meaning. These terms when verbalized or written convey ideas between individuals and groups. Yet, it is impossible to express a feeling or idea accurately, as words do not exist for everything. It too is difficult for most to accept that no one ever truly understands them when they convey a thought. This aspect of the human condition explains why words play a major role in emotional pollution. Chapter 3 explores this idea.

Words and Emotional Pollution

Since the beginning of time, human beings have developed systems of communication to interact with each other. Initially, gestures conveyed emotions related to basic survival instincts (Pinker, 2007, 2002 & 1995). As time passed, cultures refined how they stood or moved while simultaneously connecting utterances with certain objects or actions. Ultimately, sequences of sounds became associated with an object, like the word *deer* used to label a brown animal with antlers that could run and jump. These terms for people, places and things provided a way for individuals to make sense of the world around them. Oral language patterns further evolved as new discoveries and disciplines created words and phrases to explain various functions and theories (McWhorter, 1998). For instance, in the 13th century, the word *table* was created to represent "a piece of furniture with a flat top and legs." In the 14th, the definition expanded to include the "arrangement of numbers or other figures on a tabular surface for convenience"; later, (1866) in United States political verbiage, it means to "lay aside for future consideration" (Merriam-Webster Dictionary, 2017). In spite of the multiple definitions of *table*, most adults can determine its meaning based on the context in which it is used. That is not always the case, as some words do not represent something tangible. One such example is the word *selfish*. It was invented by Presbyterians in the 1630s to mean, "excessively or exclusively concerned with oneself; seeking or concentrating on one's own advantage, pleasure, or well-being without regard for others" (Merriam-Webster Dictionary, 2017). More recently, (1976) Richard Dawkins in his book the *Selfish Gene*, referred to it as "being an actively repetitive sequence of nucleic acid that serves no known function; genetic material solely concerned with its own replication." The question then is what does the word *selfish* actually mean? This lack of clarity often results in emotional pollution.

The more subjective the meaning of a word, the greater likelihood emotional pollution is associated with it. A prime example is the word *love*. People say they love someone while at times treating them badly. How can this be? In addition, how can a feeling of love be present if someone dislikes a person's actions? For that matter, what specific behaviors are acts of love? The many possible answers to these questions point out how differences in personal experiences result in a lack of consensus as to what words mean. When that is the case, emotional pollution is emitted as people try to overcome the unsettling feelings associated with not understanding something. As this occurs, words provide comfort for those communicating them while at times promoting distress for those hearing or reading them. This complex evolving dynamic leads to the ongoing creation and emission of emotional pollution.

Emotional pollution is more common in certain parts of speech. Words representing persons, places or things create fewer pollutants. For example, most people would agree as to what a house or car is. However, when nouns become action words (verbs) they are less tangible, thus, increasing the chance of emotional pollution. Examples are sentences like; the *objects* were large, square and bulky (Noun). The attorney *objects* to that line of questioning (Verb). The *permit* allows food service (Noun). John's mother *permits* him to go on a trip (verb). My *face* reflects my emotions (Noun). Students *face* challenges every day (Verb). These declarative statements (participles) show how words can be used in a number of ways to convey meaning. Other verbs, like *jog* and *run*, may also result in differences in interpretation and understanding. What some might consider a jog is a run for others. In addition, words describing nouns and verbs often trigger emotional pollution. These adjectives and adverbs increase the chance someone does not understand the intended meaning of what is said or read. Table One and Two provide information regarding adjectives and adverbs.

Table One: Adjectives (Jannayi, 2020)

Adjective Categories	Definition	Example
Quantitative	Provide information regarding how many.	There are nine planets in the solar system.

Demonstrative	Specify pronouns like "*that*", "*these*" and "*those.*"	I like that type of car.
Descriptive	Describe both nouns and pronouns.	The little puppy ran across the street.
Interrogative	Indicate the question types regarding wh's like "*what?*", "*which?*" and "*whose?*"	Whose umbrella is this?
Possessive	Describe where the object belongs.	Where is my money?
Articles	Specify the nouns that are particular or general. *A*, *an*, and *the*, are the articles.	The birdcage is open.
Distributive	Point out a particular type of object.	Jim can write on either side of the paper.
Indefinite	Something is neither accurate nor definite about the count of the objects. Like *some*, *many* and *much*.	There are many outstanding athletes playing soccer.

After reviewing the adjective categories, descriptive and indefinite are most likely to elicit the creation and emission of emotional pollution. Words considered articles and interrogatives are less apt to do so.

Table Two: Adverbs (Jannayi, 2020)

Adverb Types	Purpose	Example
Time	Provides information when an action takes place	We recently sold a gold ring.

Place	Indicates where an action is happening	We went into the grocery store and there were people everywhere.
Manner	Informs how an action is done	The old man neatly placed his clothes in the closet.
Degree	Explains the level of intensity related to an action, adjective or another adverb	I am so excited to receive my first real paycheck.
Frequency	Denotes how often an action occurs	They always seem to talk about their dogs.

The adverb types most likely to result in emotional pollution include manner, degree and frequency.

In spite of Jannayi and other scholars' attempts to create neat and orderly adjective categories and adverb types, words cannot be easily placed in a typology. Instead, word meanings are complicated by the context in which they are used and the experiences of those hearing and reading them. A recent example is the flooding that occurred in Houston, Texas. Some reporters described it using terms such as *extensive, massive, historical, unbelievable, tragic,* and *life changing.* For families who have lived through something similar those terms may be accurate; for others they are not. Other less obvious word selection differences are noticed when individuals discuss and write about paintings, rainbows, books and vacations. When thinking more about words, parts of speech, and emotional pollution, one can generally conclude that words categorized as nouns create the least amount of emotional pollution followed by verbs, adverbs and adjectives.

Over time, some words have become emotionally loaded.

They represent an image or a series of events generating intense feelings that result in emotional pollution. The word *problem* is an example. When someone says, "I have a problem" the listener normally reacts based on their level of emotional closeness. For instance, if they have had many shared positive experiences, they are more apt to empathize and provide comfort. On the other hand, if a limited bond exists between them little support is given. When that is the case, the word *problem* is likely to trigger in the listener something negative that happened to them. This pattern of behavior is noticed when someone ends a close relationship. As the individual discusses their "breakup" with family and friends, limited caring at times is demonstrated since many seem to not want to think about their own past or current relationship difficulties. Meanwhile, the person experiencing it frequently hears avoidance type clichés like, "you just have to move on" or "it just was not meant to be." Granted, these statements are well intended; nevertheless, they are emotional pollutants as they meet the needs of those verbalizing them while creating additional discomfort for the person experiencing the breakup.

A number of other variables play a role in the link between words and emotional pollution. The most obvious is the tone in which a word is communicated. In the United States, the louder, the more likely it represents a feeling of discontent, frustration or anger. Rate is another consideration. If someone speaks slower or faster than their normal speech pattern, their level of contemplation or urgency may represent the intensity of emotions felt at a particular moment. At a more abstract level, if a term is frequently used in a specific situation, it often becomes the norm for how people interact. This communication characteristic provides the foundation for future relationships. For instance, if individuals share common beliefs and language patterns they are more likely to develop a friendship. In contrast, when children and adults differ in cultural or economic backgrounds, a lack of shared experiences may result in misunderstandings and limited interactions. Lastly, and perhaps most importantly, physical health effects word selection. If someone does not feel well, words representing a negative mood are communicated. Examples are present when listening to people talk about their health, money and family. These intense feelings as well increase the chance someone becomes trapped in the emotional pollution cycle. When that is the case, children and adults use words to lessen their discomfort and pain.

Now that the purpose of words, subjectivity of meaning, and emotionally loaded terms have been briefly discussed, a number of other related ideas need mentioning. One is if people consistently associate a word with something they can see; they are less likely to emit emotional pollution in response to it. The object simply becomes an environmental fixture or constant in which they think little about. Another consideration is the frequency in which a word or phrase is used. The more often, the greater chance people become aware and comfortable with its meaning. A current example is the phrase, "It is what it is." Differences in gender, age and background also lead to multiple interpretations of word meanings, thus, increasing the probability of emotional pollution. Additionally, how people react to words influence how others respond to them. For example, if an expression results in a sense of discomfort, adults are more likely to verbalize something that creates uneasiness in others. Lastly, emotional pollution affects a person's reading ability. The greater the amount of pollutants experienced, the more apt someone struggles to read. When that is the case, individuals make assumptions about persons, places and things to guide their actions.

Words, Assumptions and Emotional Pollution

Words representing and describing human emotion create large amounts of emotional pollution. The reason is the ambiguity associated with their meanings. An example is the word *guilt.* Guilt is defined as a feeling of worry or unhappiness related to having done something wrong-causing harm to another person (Merriam-Webster Dictionary, 2017). These negative sensations sometimes arise when adults care for their aging parents. Once they die, many struggle with guilt-ridden thoughts such as, "I should have spent more time with mom." I should not have become so upset when dad did not do as his doctor told him." Another complex emotion-based term is *contentment.* It is defined as a state of being happy and satisfied (Merriam-Webster Dictionary, 2017). This broad and ambiguous description adds to the ongoing confusion as to what the word actually means. For most, the question then becomes what experiences lead to a sense of contentment. A lack of clarity in meaning is also present in a number of other words used to describe emotions. Some of which include *fear, shame, sadness, disillusioned, joyful, compassionate, empathetic, critical* and *forgiving.*

People make assumptions about persons, places and things when it is not clear what words mean. An assumption is something believed to be true or probably true that is not known to be true (Merriam-Webster Dictionary, 2017). What does that mean? Who determines how someone should feel or act in a given situation? Also, what happens when children or adults do not know the expectations, and if they do, they are unable to meet them? Answers to these and similar type questions are based on the frequency assumptions enter consciousness. Logically, the more often, the greater likelihood they are believed. Certain words perpetuate the creation and use of assumptions. The word *power* is an example. In a capitalistic society, power is usually represented in hierarchal structures that divide people into groups based on some arbitrary criteria. At each level, an authority figure creates an atmosphere in which certain information governs actions. Those who express differing viewpoints are in danger of losing their job. Freud (1933) provided another theory as to why individuals make assumptions. He implied that the emotions of fear, shame and guilt experienced during the first five-years of life contribute to future problems. As these difficulties arise, assumptions help children and adults overcome them.

Assumptions act as a form of self-protection. An example occurs when teaching college students preparing to become teachers. Many have difficulties making the connection between theories of human development and teaching practices. When attempting to help them do so, some become defensive while simultaneously relying on assumptions to gain comfort. This impulse-based pattern of behavior and subsequent lack of openness to new ideas creates an environment where words with negative meanings and connotations are communicated. Sentences containing terms and phrases like *cannot, untrue, deficit, lack, harm, problem, futile, illness, just your opinion, and never seen before* are common. Another observation is how assumptions are sometimes used to offset uncomfortable feelings towards others. Statements like, "I am sure he did not mean it that way" or "she must be having a bad day" are examples. Assumptions also provide quick and simple answers to complex problems. This indoctrinated oversimplification process is a form of self-preservation.

Assumptions are one of the major reasons why emotional pollution exists. This is because no two people have the same genetic and experiential background. Children and adults therefore vary in their perception and interpretation of what they encounter. An example occurs when Ann and George are walking together in the neighborhood. When turning the corner onto an adjacent street, flies are swarming an animal carcass on the road. For Ann, her visual memory causes her to think it is a squirrel. George believes it is a cat or opossum. The flies also cause Ann to move to the opposite side of the road as George's curiosity leads him to move closer. These contrasts in how Ann and George react to a shared experience are a natural part of the human condition. However, over time, Ann and George's experiences will cause them to differ in their assumptions about persons, places and things. This will lead to the creation and emission of various forms and levels of emotional pollution in the future. From a broader point of view, assumptions help adults gain a sense of being-grounded in an environment that makes sense to them. When that being the norm, individual and collective actions are shaped more by emotion than intellect. That is the reason why most people rely on gut feelings rather than science to guide their decisions. Sameness, simplicity, and ongoing emotional pollution occur as a result. In addition, a person's verbalizations reflect their collective assumptions. Words therefore help individuals feel better while at the same time often creating difficulties for others. The emotional pollution cycle continues just as it has in the past and will in the future.

Code Switching

Code switching is another linguistic contributor to emotional pollution. It consists of changing nonverbal and verbal communication styles based on what is socially acceptable in a particular context. For instance, certain behavioral norms exist for how an employee should discuss an issue with their boss. Other setting-based examples include the way in which groups of friends talk about a movie, a branch of the military communicating about a new procedure, or coach trying to motivate their team. Code switching usually serves two purposes. One is for children and adults to meet their immediate needs. This self-centered approach results in emotional pollution. Code switching also helps individuals feel accepted and valued. Nevertheless, the need to "fit in" often leads to a level of conformity in which adults voluntarily relinquish a part of their identity. When that is the case, many of their actions reflect an overwhelming need to be liked.

A number of outcomes result from code switching. The most significant is misunderstandings. A recent example occurred when a prominent politician discussed the inner-city unemployment rate. Many interpreted his remarks as using code words to speak negatively about adult males of color even though he said that was not his intent. Regrettably, for him, an inordinate amount of time was spent analyzing and discussing word choices rather than the merits of his proposal. These types of difficulties often result in derogatory comments that divide rather than unite people. This is a major reason why so many adults have limited empathy and compassion toward others. Another issue is the anxiety associated with not knowing for sure what words and actions are appropriate in a particular setting. To offset the uncomfortable feelings, assumptions and generalizations guide statements like, "if you belong to that group, you must be a hard worker" or "I try to kill people with kindness." What does either of those comments actually mean? Without a clear consensus, emotional pollution often leads to word choices and voice tones insensitive to others. Code switching is also present in organizations. This is reflected in the unwritten rules governing how employees respond to their immediate supervisor's phone call, text or email. The frequency in which code switching occurs also indicates the level of fear associated with those in positions of power. Logically, the more often it happens, the larger the amount. From another point of view, how an individual communicates sometimes reflects their social, institution or corporate status. For most, they adopt similar nonverbal and oral language patterns to "fit in" with their peers while at the same time trying to impress others in order to remain in their current position or advance their standing. This characteristic of code switching is learned in many of the same ways as academic subjects like reading and math.

Children learn code switching by observing and listening to what is happening around them. Then, as they begin to develop their vocabulary, they are taught how to communicate in certain contexts. For instance, most preschoolers have heard mom say, "Don't you see mommy is talking to another adult, so don't butt in and talk until we're finished." Other common examples are words children learn to use when referring to gender (terms assigned boys and girls), race (Caucasian and people of color) and socioeconomic level (rich, wealthy, poor and destitute). A number of other code-switching concepts were recently illustrated in a Dennis the Menace cartoon (Ketcham, 2017). Dennis and his father appear to be entertaining a guest. They are sitting on the sofa when Dennis says to the middle-aged man, "Can I see your other face?" "Dad says you have two!" In response, Dennis' dad looks downward as he covers his mouth perhaps indicating he is shocked and embarrassed by what his son just said. In this instance like many others, Dennis has to learn how to determine situation-specific norms for appropriate nonverbal and verbal communication. Some things he might be taught to ask himself before speaking include: who is present (gender, age, and level of power or authority) what is the setting (formal or informal), why is the conversation occurring (motivation), and what are the experiences of those participating. If Dennis can accurately answer these questions and adapt his language patterns accordingly, a number of outcomes might result. The most obvious is an increased chance of gaining social capital. For instance, if he becomes more sensitive towards others, he may acquire a variety of friends. This perhaps could help him obtain a certain job or become acquainted with someone whom becomes his life partner.

As Dennis becomes older, schools, places of worship and the media will continue to educate him on the importance of code switching. These lessons will teach him how certain thoughts cannot be communicated because they are socially inappropriate.

Instead, Dennis will learn the importance of using words to "mask" or "cover up" feelings and ideas about a particular subject. He too may ultimately realize someday that code switching does not promote honesty but rather is a form of self-preservation in which words are used to influence others. For instance, he may uncover in order to obtain what he wants, he will have to identify and conform to certain behavioral expectations. In most situations, the extent and degree Dennis does so will parallel the level of emotional pollution experienced at a particular moment. The greater the amount, the more likely he is guarded and deliberate in the way he communicates. Now that his formative years have ended, Dennis is equipped with a variety of communication skills needed to live in an evolving culture containing vast amounts of emotional pollution.

Inner Voice: Words and Emotional Pollution

Human beings have an ongoing internal dialogue guiding thoughts and actions. This subconscious and conscious state consists of words reflecting the frequency and extent of an individuals' struggle with self-esteem. Self-esteem is the value and worth placed on self. It is usually associated with the fulfillment of one's needs. At the most basic level, some children and adults have an internal dialogue consisting mainly of words associated with food and shelter. For those more fortunate, a sense of belonging is sought. This search for acceptance often results in communicating in ways similar to others. Another contributor to self-esteem is the type and quality of interactions with others. This begins in infancy when parents care for their child. As time passes, siblings, friends, teachers, coaches, life partners, employers and co-workers reinforce or alter to some degree the existing internal narrative. These personal relationships certainly influence how someone develops; however, it is also important to consider what might happen if something is not experienced. For instance, a number of scholars suggest children need physical touch and encouragement as they grow and develop. Without it, their struggle with self-esteem may occur more frequently or intensify based on certain environmental stimuli. An example is noticed in the way in which some adults cope with stress. Instead of experiencing and accepting their emotions at a given moment, they push down or suppress them. By doing so, they feel better while at the same time becoming almost numb to their own feelings. As this coping strategy becomes their emotional norm, many are likely to have an ongoing negative inner voice.

Culture plays a significant role in an individual's inner voice. It provides the frame of reference as to what society deems as successful. For example, in the United States commercial advertisements portray success as a certain appearance, educational level, vocation, and material possessions. For those who fit the description, their inner voice is more likely to consist of positive words than those who do not. As these external variables shape and guide internal narratives, emotional pollution is created and emitted as children and adults try to obtain things they think will make them happy. A number of other cultural characteristics need mentioning regarding the inner voice. One is how no single or group of variables determines it. Therefore, it is statistically impossible to have a high degree of confidence in any conclusions drawn about or from someone's innermost thoughts.

Second, individuals have their own unique personal narrative. Causal relationships are not possible when discussing a dynamic evolving entity (human being) within an ongoing changing context (culture). Moreover, if someone attempts to do so, he or she is overgeneralizing information. Little emphasis is placed on human dignity when that happens. Lastly, certain words in an individual's inner voice promote physical and emotional health while others do not.

Words associated with emotional pollution increase the amount of time someone has a negative inner voice. This typically results in a pessimistic mood. As this emotional state arises and dominates thoughts, individuals create a personal narrative shaped more by negative rather than positive feelings. These uncomfortable sensations affect the frequency and intensity (volume) of the inner voice. For instance, if a child is consistently told they are incapable of doing something, they eventually believe it is true. In contrast, if constantly immersed with positive comments, they are more like to develop a false sense of ability. In either scenario, emotional pollution presents itself in words communicating some level of fear, anxiety and depression. When that occurs, adults tend to gravitate towards others who have similar perspectives. By doing so, they gain a sense of belonging while at the same time placing themselves in a certain energy cycle. For instance, those with a negative mood attract others who are negative. They then normally add to and reinforce (feed off) each other's attitude. Another related issue is how some words lead to thoughts and actions reflecting a distorted view of reality. For example, at any point in time, a number of adolescents feel that no one truly cares about them. Then, when entering adulthood, many realize how awful that feeling was and they do not want others to experience it. In response, some enter helping professions. These individuals are also prone to overreact to what they perceive as uncaring actions. They too often struggle to understand why others are not as compassionate or empathetic as they are.

A person's inner voice affects their health. The more positive words thought or spoken, the greater likelihood someone has a strong immune system. In contrast, terms triggering emotional pollution result in physical vulnerability. For instance, as joints and muscles begin or more frequently hurt negative words often represent an individual's emotional state. When that happens, changes in sleep patterns perpetuate the intensity and length of time someone experiences discomfort and pain. This increased susceptibility to emotional pollution as well sometimes leads to poor food choices, substance abuse and a myriad of other actions detrimental to health. Then, as days, months, and years pass, the accumulation of negative feelings often causes someone to believe they have little control in their life. This sense of helplessness leads to an inner voice containing limited positive thoughts towards self, others and the events occurring in the environment. Unfortunately, this personal perspective lessens the likelihood someone experiences joy and happiness. It too may ultimately contribute to a shorter lifespan.

A person's inner voice determines the extent in which they are happy. More specifically, it influences how they view themselves, their relationships, and the level of enjoyment felt in response to certain experiences. For most, the frequency and degree of emotional pollution encountered parallels the amount of time with a positive or negative internal narrative. High levels lead to words indicating a limited sense of control in life. These terms also represent a point of view in which someone is just trying to survive in a world that makes little sense to them. As these feelings of hopelessness arise and evolve, children and adults exhibit actions to feel better while at the same time creating difficulties for those around them. Those affected then demonstrate similar types of behavior. This emotional pollution cycle reflects the ongoing struggle individuals have with their inner voice.

Chapter Summary

This chapter discussed words and emotional pollution. Historically, words have been created to label and describe things in the environment. These terms enable children and adults to make sense of the world around them. Words also play a major role in the creation and emission of emotional pollution. For instance, the more subjective a terms definition, the greater likelihood misunderstandings occur. As these difficulties arise, pollutants are often emitted as individuals interact. Adults too tend to make assumptions about persons, places and things when it is not clear what certain words mean. By doing so, they gain a sense of safety and security. Assumptions though perpetuate the emotional pollution cycle as they help individuals meet their immediate needs while at the same time creating difficulties for others. As this dynamic unfolds, a distorted view of reality develops in which adults think mainly about themselves. This pattern of behavior is the reason why individual and collective actions have had limited success addressing issues such as, extreme hunger, violence and inequality.

Code switching was then presented as another linguistic contributor to emotional pollution. It consists of changing nonverbal and verbal communication patterns based on what is socially acceptable in a particular context. This characteristic of the human condition leads to varying levels of emotional pollution because no one knows for sure appropriate words and actions for all situations. An example is the differing definitions of manners. Actions perceived as appropriate by some might be seen by others as arrogance, aloofness or pushy behavior. This lack of clarity in meaning often results in words being used to "mask" or "cover up" certain feelings and ideas. The extent and degree in which this occurs parallels the level of emotional pollution experienced at a particular moment. The greater the amount, the more likely someone tightens their "mask" in order to avoid certain feelings. In other words, they become deliberate, guarded, and calculated in the way they communicate. Code switching therefore does not promote honesty but rather is a form of self-preservation.

An individual's inner voice was discussed next. This subconscious and conscious state consists of words from past and current experiences. For most people, feelings related to survival act as the foundation for the inner voice. Logically then, emotional pollution adds to the amount of time in which insecurity and self-doubt circulate within the mind. A person's self-esteem reflects their innermost thoughts. Those who frequently struggle with how they feel about themselves are more likely to have experienced various forms of emotional pollution. The inner voice also affects a person's mood. This state of being not only influences how an individual perceives themselves, their experiences, and the world in general, it too significantly contributes to lifestyle choices that promote or hinder the quality of life.

In the end, words act paradoxically. They help gain a sense of order while at the same time creating disorder. Children and adults need to be able to explain the things occurring around them; words help them to do so. Still, differences in genetic endowments and personal experiences result in a lack of clarity as to what some words mean. This difficulty often creates misunderstandings between and among individuals. As this form of disorder unfolds, the emotional pollution cycle continues as those experiencing discomfort and pain communicate in ways to feel better while simultaneously polluting the environment for those around them. This uniquely human process often leads to the creation and dissemination of information perceived as propaganda. Chapter Four explores this form of emotional pollution.

Chapter 4

Propaganda

Emotional pollution is the innate, environmental or combination of elements negatively affecting thoughts and actions. This always present but rarely discussed environmental pollutant occurs when children and adults experience discomfort and pain. As these uncomfortable internal sensations arise, actions are exhibited to feel better. Those adversely affected by them then demonstrate similar types of behavior. This emotional pollution cycle happens within the context of communication. For instance, when Sara and Morgan are talking, if Morgan makes Sara uncomfortable, she more than likely will try to change the subject or end the conversation. In most instances, this pattern of behavior does not promote emotional closeness. Instead, it creates a cultural atmosphere where individuals and groups try to influence others to satisfy their own needs. This complex and fluid characteristic of the human condition is captured in the term *propaganda*. The form of emotional pollution discussed in the upcoming chapter.

Propaganda

Propaganda is subconscious or conscious actions by an individual or group to shape behavior. It naturally occurs as children and adults try to influence those around them in order to meet their needs and wants. In the past, tribal leaders protected themselves by misleading hunters and gatherers to where food, water and shelter were located. During this period, word of mouth transmitted information. Propaganda also affected the power structure within groups. Those perceived as having the most physical strength usually shaped the thoughts and behaviors of others. In extreme cases, children and adults who did not respect or conform to what was said were harmed. As time passed and life became less physically demanding, propaganda became more of a covert activity. Lasswell (1971) indicated it focused on three tactical objectives. One is to arouse the interest of specific groups. The goal is to use symbols such as stories and parables, rumors and pictures to create a belief that certain information is true. In world wars, balloons were strategically released to do this. The second objective is to invalidate troublesome ideas. Vulnerable adults like those who are hungry, without shelter or generally disillusioned are helped in order to gain their support in shaping perspectives. Lastly, propagandists try to control the flow of information to prevent the uncovering of the truth. Those who present opposing points of view are discredited. Their ideas are commonly labeled conspiracy theories. Regardless of what the purpose might be, successful propaganda depends on the management of opinions and attitudes by the direct manipulation of social suggestion (Lasswell, 1971). In other words, propaganda is a form of emotional pollution used to create and intensify disagreement, anxiety, nervousness, depression and a host of other uncomfortable feelings. It too results in a cultural atmosphere in which fear and anxiety cause individuals to spend more time with a negative rather than positive mood. Those with this perspective are more likely to create and emit emotional pollution.

Lasswell's ideas are still used today to develop and spread propaganda. It normally begins with a media report of an extreme event. Once the majority becomes aware of the incident or situation, repeated exposure causes many to believe the commentary surrounding it. This legitimization process is accelerated if those in positions of power discuss it frequently. When that is the case, the new information is presented as a fact or logical reason why certain actions are needed. This sequence of events often occurs when newscasters discuss topics like economics, policing, elder care, and the treatment of animals. Four variables play a role in determining if propaganda is believed. One is the age of those involved; the younger, the more likely something is accepted as true. Especially, when an adult in whom they have an emotional connection shares the information. Usually, this is a parent, extended family member, teacher or coach. Second is intellectual ability. The more abstract an individuals' thinking, the greater the number of ideas arise regarding different points of view. Propaganda is less likely accepted as an answer to a question when someone has this ability. In contrast, those who think concretely often accept something as true without much thought. Third is the level of fear someone experiences. If a person is innately predisposed to be fearful, they are more susceptible to propaganda. The same is true for those who have experienced adverse childhood experiences or in a state of toxic stress. Lastly, if someone has a strong need for belonging, he or she tends to adopt similar views of those in a particular group. This often results in the spread of propaganda.

Propaganda and science are interconnected. At the most basic level, propaganda originates with an observation, followed by an idea, ending with some theory how to shape the thoughts and actions of others. This sequence of events parallels the scientific method. It begins with a hypothesis, followed by the identification of dependent and independent variables, descriptions of methodology, and discussions of findings and conclusions (Kuhn, 1962). Study results however are skewed to some degree by emotional pollution. Often, this is associated with the preconceived assumptions of the author or those financially supporting the research. Nevertheless, from a practical point of view, without private sector investments many academics would be unemployed as universities value those who are able to obtain research grants. This reliance on external funding inadvertently promotes the creation, promotion, and dissemination of information that might not be accurate. Some of which is used as propaganda. Another science related issue is its emphasis placed on quantification. When the majority value something based on numbers, individuals and society in general are more susceptible to propaganda. Daily examples are opinion polls surveying the attitudes of citizens regarding a particular issue, medical tests determining if a person's blood work is normal and financial advisors promoting the need to have a certain amount of money to live comfortably in retirement. Topics such as these highlight how someone can easily mislead others by manipulating numbers. Science for that reason is a common tool used by propagandist to shape the perspectives of others.

Hierarchal social structures reflect how propaganda is used to maintain order. Those at the top are the elite; others are the rank-and-file. Elites preserve their power and dominance by manipulating symbols, controlling supplies, and applying violence (Lasswell, 1965). Today, money is associated with elevated status. Those who have it significantly influence the policies and procedures governing public and private entities. Having means also contributes to the acquisition of social capital. Relationships with certain individuals or belonging to a particular group often lead to desired personal and professional opportunities. This class-based aspect of the human condition creates vast amounts of emotional pollution. For example, those at the pinnacle of the social structure try to keep their position through political donations or corporate policies. On the other end of the economic spectrum, adults with barely enough to survive protect themselves in any way possible. By doing so, they often instinctively emotionally pollute the environment they are in. Those in the middle are also vulnerable because of their desire to live a certain lifestyle. Their fear of losing what they have often causes them to place an overemphasis on work. In the end, no matter where someone lands on the hierarchy, propaganda is an ongoing fear-based variable shaping thoughts and actions.

A number of other thoughts regarding propaganda and emotional pollution need mentioning. One is how all information can be considered propaganda. It is a societal constant reflecting how genetic and experiential differences result in varying perspectives. This is evident when siblings discuss an experience they shared. In most instances, the emotions associated with the event results in memories that differ. The question then becomes what really did happen on vacation, at the funeral, during the ball game or car accident. Truth regarding any matter becomes debatable. Emotional pollution is often the consequence of these differences in recollections. The way in which words are used to convey ideas is another propaganda consideration. An example is the word *justice*. This socially constructed term is frequently communicated but rarely defined. Without a clear consensus of meaning, multiple interpretations lead to the creation and emission of emotional pollution. Division rather than unity is the normal outcome. Propagandists also rely on linguistic confusion to influence others. For instance, information from something written in the 1940's may lead to unintended misinterpretations due to cultural changes over time. In addition, changes in the pace in which generations live influences the degree in which material is understood. The faster, the more likely someone overlooks or misinterprets information. Propagandists as well promote a "whirlwind culture" where individuals struggle to complete their daily activities. These difficulties cause many to be easily led by a charismatic leader. In addition, overt propaganda is a lie. When individuals purposely communicate something other than the truth, they not only mislead others but also pollute the context it is shared. This type of action is usually justified based on some comment like; "it is for the greater good" or "what would happen if they truly knew what was going on." Lastly, the mathematical concept of probability makes it possible to be less vulnerable to propaganda. More specifically, primary and secondary sources of information can be studied to determine the likelihood of something being true. Of course, the innate, environmental or combination of elements comprising emotional pollution plays a role in how data is collected, interpreted and valued.

Sources of Propaganda

Emotional communities are sources of propaganda. They consist of groups of people who share fundamental assumptions, values, goals, feelings and accepted modes of expression

(Rosenwein, 2006). Emotional communities can be further thought of as large circles within which are smaller ones. In each, individuals represent a constellation of emotions reflecting ideologies, theories and actions. Bronfenbrenner's (1979) ecological theory of development described a similar type of environment as a set of nested structures, each inside the next. At the innermost level are the immediate settings in which children function. This can be a home or school. The next looks beyond single locations to the relationship between them. For instance, how learning is impacted by neighborhood experiences. The third is yet further away; it explores how development is affected by events occurring in locations in which someone is not present. The work experiences of parents naturally affect their children. Finally, within any culture, an organizational framework reflects common values that are distinctively different from others. Bronfenbrenner (1997) as well implied life reflects a history of events, beliefs and relationships embedded in a changing social, cultural and economic environment.

With Rosenwein's and Bronfenbrenner's theories in mind, it is important to accept that children and adults' function within a multifaceted evolving culture. Human development does not take place in single aspects taken out of context. Instead, it is a series of complex dynamic interactions occurring simultaneously in a nonlinear fashion. How a person changes throughout life is therefore not an accumulation of outcomes but rather a process of restructuring subsystems and the whole structure within biological and social boundaries. More specifically, human beings develop within an equilibrium model consisting of an initial state of harmonious existence, emergence of some disruption, and time dependent movement toward the restoration of a state of harmony (Bronfenbrenner, 1995). Propaganda plays a significant role in this process. For most people, it triggers psychological discomfort and pain – the disruption. As these feelings surface and intensify, emotional pollution is created and emitted while individuals try to obtain a new state of equilibrium. This ongoing search for a sense of physical and psychological balance is influenced by the propaganda associated with social institutions.

Propaganda is present in families. This is obvious when considering the differences in authoritative, authoritarian, permissive, and rejecting/neglecting/uninvolved child rearing practices. Authoritative parents have strong emotional bonds with their children. They listen to concerns, give reasons for rules and allow democratic decision-making. Authoritarian parents on the other hand, love their kids but are not openly affectionate. Youth in these types of families usually do not observe adult models of emotion but rather are supposed to be mature and obedient. If not, punishments are harsh. Permissive parents have few rules and expect little in the way of appropriate conduct. Children in this situation are often insecure and lack purposeful behavior. Rejecting, neglecting, uninvolved parents do not care much about anything affecting their kids. When that is the case, young people are in a constant struggle to meet their most basic physical and emotional needs (Baumrind 2005). After thinking about these parenting styles, a child's degree of vulnerability to propaganda is connected to need fulfillment. The greater the need, the more likely they are easily led to believe information. Those having rejecting, neglecting, and uninvolved parents would be the most at risk followed by permissive, authoritarian, and authoritative. On an individual level, adults providing children with a sense of safety and security are likely to influence their thoughts and actions.

Extended family members contribute to the creation and spread of propaganda. Aunts, uncles and grandparents often reinforce what a child has been previously taught. In most families, their level of influence is based on the frequency and quality of interactions. Logically, the more often, and stronger the emotional bond, the greater chance information is believed. As a result, young people often adopt the religious and political viewpoints of their family. Relatives similar in age also influence each other's thinking. This usually occurs through digital platforms that allow opportunities to share experiences. For instance, a teenager in North Dakota can play a videogame in real-time with a cousin living in Florida. Conversations while competing effect how they think about issues important to them. Other occasions to share propaganda are present during special events such as, holidays and birthdays.

A family's economic status plays a role in propaganda. The greater the amount of resources available the less likely inaccurate information is believed to be true. This class-based aspect of the human condition begins with the quality of prenatal care and continues throughout life. For example, the number of books read to a preschooler not only nurtures communication development but also promotes future literacy skills. Then, as children begin to read, they have opportunities to explore a variety of materials rather than relying only on what others tell them. They too are apt to have access to information available on various technology platforms. Money also provides children and adults opportunities to learn while traveling to various locations throughout the world. Vacations generally improve the mood of those who can temporarily escape the mundane aspects of daily life. As a result, they may be less vulnerable to the fear associated with propaganda. From another point of view, historically, families with human, financial, and social capital have created and spread propaganda for their own benefit. Examples are evident in the oil (Rockefeller); steel (Carnegie), automobile (Ford) and banking (Morgan) industries. Now that we have briefly examined the primary social institutions creating and spreading propaganda, it is time to explore two others: education and media.

At the heart of any society is an education commitment that affords members the opportunity to stretch their minds to full capacity. Education is important because of not only what it contributes to individuals but also the value added to the general quality of life within communities. Historically, in the United States, an industrial model has been used to guide formal education. This assembly line approach is reflected in the design of grade levels, student codes of conduct, curriculum, and policies governing attendance, length of school day and year, and graduation requirements. Two teaching approaches have also been traditionally used: direct instruction and constructivist. In direct instruction, students are relatively passive in the learning process as the teacher does most of the talking while they sit quietly at their desks listening, responding when called upon, and completing assigned tasks. In contrast, constructivism focuses on inquiry-based learning. Teachers pose various types of questions to guide and support students as they use existing knowledge to explore and uncover new information. Still, regardless of what instructional approach is used, propaganda is taught in schools. This is obvious when thinking about the differences in historical accounts of people, places and events. For instance, in some textbooks, Native Americans are portrayed as savages while others describe them as indigenous groups trying to protect their land. Other conflicting stories are present when studying topics such as slavery, economics and war. Another curriculum issue is how teachers and students are conditioned to believe something is important only to the extent it is measured on a standardized achievement test. An example is the differing amounts of instructional time allocated for certain types of math problems. Extracurricular activities also spread propaganda. This occurs when group leaders interact with participants. In some cases, coaches model yelling and the use of profanity as a form of motivation or stress the quantity rather than quality of practice. These types of behaviors often continue when some players become coaches.

An educator's frame of reference plays a role in the spread of propaganda. For example, the school experiences of teachers influence how they teach. This is evident in some of the comments of pre-service teachers. They state, "I turned out ok, so how I was taught must have been alright." "So, when I become a teacher, I really do not need to know this information." Another related issue is the level of content knowledge an educator has in a certain area. If a self-contained elementary school teacher intellectually struggles with a subject, he or she is more likely to communicate inaccurate information. This frequently occurs in math, social studies and science. A number of other characteristics of educators affect the extent in which propaganda is taught. One is the level of collective intellectual curiosity present in a school. The more, the greater likelihood teachers read and participate in professional development opportunities. By doing so, they increase the accuracy of information presented to students. Another is the personal wellness of educators. If teachers are physically and mentally healthy, they are more likely to reflect upon student interactions, lesson effectiveness, and instructional strategies. They too probably self-monitor biases while assessing and instructing their students. Lastly, is an educators' desire to collaborate. If teachers are willing to work together and learn from each other, the amount of propaganda spread decreases.

Students share propaganda with each other. Most adolescents for example rely on peers for information rather than adults. Teenagers as well tend to form and join cliques in order to obtain some sense of belonging. In many situations, to remain a member they adopt ideas without question. This pattern of behavior usually results in certain groups receiving elevated status based on academic ability, athletic prowess, family resources, and social capital. Regardless of what students may experience in school, some information learned is not accurate. This increases the chance that propaganda – a form of emotional pollution, will lead to a number of negative thoughts and interactions between and among individuals and groups. Some of which will manifest in actions considered to be bullying, discrimination and sexist. These types of behavior are often reinforced by information from the media.

The media influences how and what people think. Today, twenty-four-hour access to information allows individuals to have knowledge of events they previously had no idea existed.

At any moment, it is possible to obtain an update on the war in Afghanistan or view damages caused by wildfires in California or tornados in Oklahoma. This increased level of awareness results in a variety of emotion-based responses ranging from personal validation and acceptance, to a general sense of fear. In other words, adults can use social media to communicate with others having similar experiences; then, a few minutes later watch videos causing them significant levels of discomfort. Another media related matter is how some users search for stimulating visual and auditory content. Propagandists often use this ongoing need to influence and control the narrative regarding a particular topic. Political statements such as "Are you better off today, then four years ago?" or "Would you trust this person to determine when to push the button to drop a bomb" demonstrate how stimuli are manipulated to influence opinions. Political campaigns also illustrate the degree in which candidates are willing to use the media for personal gain. Of course, if a specific strategy works, it continues often as a form of emotional pollution. Examples are negative advertisements attacking the opponent; and, the subsequent comment, "I approve this message."

The way in which the media conveys information determines the propaganda associated with it. Lengthy reports along with repeated exposure (looping) increases the likelihood something is believed to be true. Money is another influential variable. The views of corporate sponsors shape how a particular incident or topic is discussed. For example, major news stories are reported differently based on the political affiliations of television stations. As these discrepancies arise, a sense of competition between points of view creates an atmosphere where an individual or group is portrayed as a winner or loser. When that happens, viewers are more apt to believe certain information in order to be associated with a winner. Lastly, chance plays a role in how the media spreads propaganda. For instance, the news cycle repeats a story until something else arises. An example is a natural disaster. People become aware of it, respond in some way (donating blood or money) and then it leaves their consciousness once another emotion-based report unfolds like the quality of drinking water (Flint, Michigan), political transgressions (Elliot Wiener), a celebrity death (Prince) or some sports scandal (Performance Enhancing Drugs).

The Internet is another source of propaganda. Information obtained from it is seldom if ever monitored for accuracy. Instead, the frequency in which users select a website often determines its location within a search engine. With that being the case, the content on page one is more frequently viewed than something found on page ten. An additional propaganda consideration is the amount of time someone has to read. With very little, adults rely on archival-based websites such as, Ask Me or WebMD to synthesize data. This approach increases the probability that money, advertising, and political views influence what is considered true. In contrast, if someone has a lot of time, reading various accounts of events and research studies may create confusion and anxiety. To offset the uncomfortable feelings, many adults rely only on certain websites to gain information. This form of digital self-insulation leads to the acceptance of information without much thought. It is also evident that even though Internet opportunities exist to conduct research, most people do not do so. Rather, they innately gravitate towards information they agree with. This characteristic of the human condition continues the evolving and dynamic process of creating and disseminating propaganda.

Social media websites also play a role in the type and amount of propaganda present at a particular point in time. For example, the number of people on Facebook or similar type-site determines the information available. The larger, the more likely inaccuracies are written, read and commented on. What is also evident is how topic discussions change beyond the intent of an individual's post. As this takes place, spontaneous digital access often leads to a series of responses perpetuating propaganda. Adults for instance sometimes search (troll) websites for information they disagree with. Once located, differing viewpoints are shared in an attempt to discredit someone in an emotion-based competition. Another social media issue is related to the links posted on personal webpages. If someone has a large following, what is on his or her page is more likely read. Social media as well provides a safe medium to share information somebody normally would not openly communicate. This, what is sometimes thought of as "hiding behind the technology," promotes the ongoing creation and sharing of propaganda – a form of emotional pollution.

Now that social institutions creating and spreading propaganda have been discussed, a number of other thoughts need mentioning. All children and adults are sources of propaganda. This naturally begins when a baby cries to gain the attention of his or her parents. As life progresses, their actions to some degree will attempt to influence others for personal gain. The term *selfish* is commonly associated with this human characteristic. In actuality, all individuals are selfish to some extent. This obviously leads to context-specific propaganda. At a more abstract level, the terms *imply* and *infer* describe how propaganda occurs within the context of human interactions. Imply is defined as what is intended to be communicated, but is not directly stated. Infer is the process of assigning meaning to what is heard or read. This nebulous dynamic is a natural barrier to emotional closeness since it is impossible to understand totally what someone else is communicating or has experienced. Lastly, feelings of discomfort and pain lead to subconscious or conscious forms of propaganda. These attempts to influence others are a form of emotional pollution used to create and intensify disagreement, anxiety, nervousness, depression and a host of other uncomfortable feelings. Propaganda also creates a cultural atmosphere in which fear is used as a form of social manipulation shaping opinions and attitudes. This normally results in individuals spending more time with a negative rather than positive mood.

In review, emotional communities are sources of propaganda. These formal and informal groups share fundamental assumptions, values, goals, feelings and accepted modes of expression (Rosenwein, 2006). For most, family is their emotional community. Parents and children develop a sense of closeness as they share experiences. This emotional bond creates an atmosphere where information discussed within the family is thought to be true. Jane will believe what her brother Bob says because she feels he cares about her. "He would never tell me something that was not true." This blind acceptance leads to the dissemination of propaganda from one generation to the next. Education is another social institution perpetuating propaganda. To some degree, inaccurate information is present in the design of grade levels, codes of conduct, length of school day and year, and graduation requirements. Differences in how textbooks portray persons, places and events also result in the design of curriculum experiences containing misinformation. Characteristics of educators as well play a role in the spread of propaganda. The information teachers learned while in school influence what they teach. If inaccuracies were a part of their experience, they are likely to share them with students. The media is another less obvious emotional community. It provides a way and ongoing opportunity for someone to gain a sense of acceptance and belonging. For instance, social media platforms help individuals' network with others who share common beliefs and interests. Yet, information obtained from the Internet has little or no level of accountability. With that being the norm, extreme points of view trigger a false sense of hope and fear. These emotions increase the probability individuals and groups believe ideas that are not true. When that occurs, the typical response is the creation of additional inaccurate information. Much of which is placed on the Internet.

Propaganda Outcomes

A number of individual and collective outcomes result from propaganda. The most significant is propaganda triggers fear. These uncomfortable feelings create an atmosphere of mistrust. When that is the case, children and adults build psychological walls for protection. As this innate process unfolds, three things normally happen. One, adults have a limited number of individuals whom they are emotionally close. This may cause them to feel no one cares about them or there must be something inherently wrong; otherwise, they would not experience such loneliness. Adults with few meaningful relationships are more prone to rely on propaganda to explain the events they are experiencing. Second, the taller or stronger the psychological wall the more likely someone depends on daily routines for a sense of safety and security. This pattern of behavior is a form of self-oppression. For example, many are reluctant to explore ideas different from their own. Innate talent remains dormant or is not nurtured to the level in which it might exist when this occurs. Lastly, psychological walls hinder someone's ability to identify and experience the beauty around them. Instead, a survival mentality causes them to overlook the natural brilliance of the environment or the positive characteristics of others.

A lack of trust leads to a number of outcomes. From a global perspective, leaders of countries create alliances to protect themselves from those perceived as not trustworthy. These relationships usually consist of shared goals and resources such as military bases, waterways, technology and information. By pooling and leveraging assets, certain nations influence the way in which people live. These ongoing associations though are impacted by propaganda. An example is how information is shared between governments. In many instances, mistrust results in allies spying on each other. When that occurs, a worldwide sense of political instability leads to the ongoing creation and spread of propaganda. Another broad issue is related to the acceptance of diversity. For most, difficulties with trust lessen the number of interactions with others. Instead, adults physically gravitate towards those who look like them. Once in their presence, a common language along with shared experiences normally determines if they remain. Often, this is linked to religious affiliation, education and economic level, and favorite past time. This type of self-insulation plays a role in creating and maintaining stereotypes based on gender, ethnicity, age, and a host of other human characteristics.

The mistrust of others is a barrier to cultural responsiveness. Defined broadly, cultural responsiveness is individual and collective actions that are sensitive to differences in language, economic and education level, and experiences among people. It focuses on promoting acceptance, and the respectful and dignified treatment of all children and adults. This social construct like many others (social justice, fairness and equality) is almost impossible to attain when an atmosphere of mistrust is present. When that is the case, most people try to protect themselves while focusing on obtaining what is in their best interest. As this happens, information enters consciousness only to the degree it affects their sense of well-being. This ego-driven pattern of behavior is one of the major reasons why vast social disparities exist today.

Laws and government regulations reflect the level of mistrust in society. In the United States, citizens to some degree willingly relinquish personal freedoms in order to gain a sense of safety. For example, motorists blindly obey state and local laws governing automobile speed, parking, and the flow of traffic. They too accept that violators should pay fines or lose the opportunity to drive. In addition, a general sense of mistrust has led to the creation of public agencies monitoring food safety, justice, water and air pollution, trade agreements, education, and working conditions. Without these forms of government oversight, many people would experience high levels of anxiety wondering if their food was contaminated or if someone might harm them if they left their home. When the majority feels the need to be protected, they become vulnerable to the propaganda created and spread by corporate and political lobbyists. These current day propagandists receive large amounts of industry (pharmaceutical, oil and gun) and special interest group (AARP and teachers unions) resources to influence federal, state and local decision-makers. Recent media reports have even suggested lawmakers rely on lobbyists to write legislation they portray as their own. Of course, when that is uncovered, it reinforces the high level of mistrust already present in society.

Truth is another issue related to mistrust. It is difficult to determine whom to believe when conflicting stories are on the Internet or reported in the local and national news. An example is global warming. Some reports indicate how plant and animal species are becoming extinct because of changes in the climate. Others do not believe global warming exists. Similar contradictions appear when studying air and water pollution, income inequality, and racial discrimination. Feelings of anxiety normally surface, and at times, intensify when adults are unsure of the answers to questions important to them. As a result, many try to avoid settings and situations creating these uncomfortable internal sensations. However, when they do interact with others, they are hesitant to communicate what they really think about a particular topic such as, religion, politics and child rearing. Another response to issues related to truth is the creation of subcultures. These groups consist of individuals who share core beliefs, communication styles, and common actions. A sense of safety, security, and personal acceptance is attained by being a member. Propagandists thrive when an atmosphere of anxiety is present. The discomfort associated with it normally causes individuals to search for simple answers to complex problems. When that is the case, various forms of propaganda can easily influence attitudes, ideas and actions.

Propaganda also plays a role in personal contentment. Propagandists try to create an atmosphere of discontent in order to shape and manage beliefs, attitudes and actions. To do so, the word *happiness* is often used. For many individuals, the question is, "What does it feel like to be happy?" Without clarity and certainty, adults are conditioned to believe that something tangible will make them happy. This mindset often results in an ongoing quest to attain what society deems of value, like a certain level of education, type of job, home or lifestyle. As adults try to meet these arbitrary standards, they usually determine their current level of happiness based on comparisons to others. This type of self-evaluation often leads to a reductionist perspective in which life is divided into parts such as, a relationship with a significant other, vocation, family, and friends. When this occurs, adults organize their experiences into categories and then place some value on them. In spite of what some counselors believe to be a helpful process, basic survival instincts cause individuals more often than not to perceive things negatively rather than positively. Most then strive for something better. This may be the reason why half of all marriages end in divorce, corporate leaders continually try to increase profits, and couples pursue larger homes.

An ongoing sense of discontentment leads to gullibility.

This is evident when researching the number of individuals participating in get-rich quick schemes, fad diets, and other similar types of activities. What is common among these actions is how emotion more so than intellect guides them. When that is the case, individuals develop a personal narrative in which they are comfortable. Unfortunately, this mindset limits the number of opportunities to meet others different from them. Personal growth is hindered when this occurs. In addition, emotion promotes an atmosphere of competition. When someone has to be the winner or loser, an-us-versus-them mentality creates division among and between individuals and groups. It too leads to a societal atmosphere in which many individuals feel that life is unfair. Lastly and perhaps most importantly, is how emotion results in more negative than positive energy. This characteristic of the human condition enables propagandists to use fear, disillusionment, and unhappiness to shape individual and collective actions.

Discontentment affects decision-making. Those who have difficulties making decisions are more prone to have a negative mood as they wonder, "Why life is so hard." To think more about this, a cardinal scale ranging from one to five might be helpful. One would represent a low level of discontentment with five being high. Those scoring a four or five would consistently struggle with problem solving. They too are more likely to believe information without much thought. Propagandists of course try to manipulate visual and auditory stimuli so individuals score high on the scale. Their efforts typically focus on ways to trigger certain emotions related to personal relationships, health, money and employment. An example is job creation. Many corporate executives use some form of propaganda to convince local and state leaders how they will benefit if their company locates in the area. Business proposals often contain the number of citizens employed, tax dollars generated, and how the general quality of life in the community improves. In return, corporations request and sometimes even demand local tax breaks on land purchases, discounts on expansion-related construction materials and equipment, as well as non-educational property tax abatements. At the state level, investment, and job creation tax credits are also frequently given to relocating industries (Griffin, 2016). When reflecting upon these common practices, a small number of individuals gain a disproportionate amount of financial benefit when the majority accepts this plan of action.

To reiterate, a number of outcomes result from propaganda. The most important is how propaganda triggers fear. When these uncomfortable internal sensations arise, many adults feel limited control over the experiences occurring in their life. This leads to the development of psychological walls. As this instinctive form of self-preservation evolves, individuals collectively become increasingly reluctant to trust each other. Many also struggle to determine what is true regarding a particular matter. With that being the societal norm, propagandists are able to manipulate information to gain the power and momentum needed to influence and control public opinion. Today, political and corporate lobbyists are the propagandists. They use money and the media to create not only an atmosphere of mistrust, but also discontent for and among individuals. In response, citizens often question if they are happy. If not, they are conditioned to believe they should look for something or someone to gain a sense of contentment. When adults adopt this mindset, they often make decisions based on what is in their best interest rather than how society might benefit. As a result, propaganda continues to be a form of emotional pollution just as it has in the past and will in the future.

Chapter Summary

This chapter discussed how propaganda is a form of emotional pollution. These subconscious and conscious actions by an individual or group, try to shape behavior. Historically, this began when someone located food and shelter. They more often than not probably provided misinformation to insure their future well-being. Then, as time passed and life became less physically demanding, propaganda evolved to covert actions intensifying fear, anxiety, depression and a host other uncomfortable internal sensations. As one might also expect, the degree in which needs are met determines susceptibility to propaganda. Adults who consistently struggle fulfilling them are the most vulnerable. Propaganda as well increases the amount of time someone has a negative mood. When that is the case, their perception of themselves and the events occurring around them often trigger actions lessening discomfort and pain. Those negatively affected then usually exhibit similar types of behavior. This propaganda driven emotional pollution cycle is the reason why many societal problems exist.

Today, propaganda develops within a sequence of events. It begins with a media report of an extreme incident or situation like a wildfire or police shooting. As citizens become aware of what happened, repeated news coverage usually triggers an emotional reaction. This state of being allows propagandists to use words strategically to shape behavior. An example is the term *tragedy*. What some might view as something terrible is an ongoing hardship for another. For others, it is only a temporary annoyance. These differences in perception lead to a culture where the majority function based on a survival mentality. This results in adults instinctively judging and assigning labels to person, places and things. That which does not fit neatly into a category creates the level of individual and collective insecurity needed for propagandists to shape behavior. Common targets of propaganda are those who look, think and act differently. Propagandists also rely on emotion to shape the connotations associated with words. *Competition* is an example. When someone has to be a winner and loser, adults become overly concerned about how others perceive them. As a result, they are easily influenced to act based on misinformation – the ultimate goal of propagandists.

Emotional communities were presented as sources of propaganda. These formal and informal groups share fundamental assumptions, values, goals, feelings and accepted modes of expression (Rosenwein, 2006). For most, family is their emotional community. As parents and children develop a sense of closeness, information shared between them is thought to be true. Education is another source of propaganda. Differences in textbook descriptions of people, places and events lead to curriculum experiences containing misinformation. Characteristics of educators as well play a role in propaganda. The information teachers learned while in school influence what they teach. If inaccuracies were a part of their experience, they are likely to share them with students. The media is another less obvious emotional community. Social media platforms enable individuals to network with others who share common beliefs and interests. This helps them attain a sense of acceptance and belonging. Information obtained from the Internet however has little or no level of accountability. With that being the norm, individuals and groups are more likely to believe something that is not true.

The chapter ends with a discussion of propaganda outcomes. Fear was presented as the most significant as it results in a culture where individuals struggle to trust each other. As a result, the truth regarding any matter is difficult to determine. With that being the case, individuals develop psychological walls as a form of self-preservation. As this instinctive process happens, information enters consciousness only to the degree it affects well-being. This ego-driven pattern of behavior is the major reason why vast disparities exist in economic, education and other quality of life indicators. Personal contentment is also impacted by propaganda. Propagandists try to create an atmosphere of discontent. To do so, the word *happiness* is often used. For many, an ongoing dilemma exists as to what it feels like. Without knowing, adults are more vulnerable to believe information without much thought. An example is someone who thinks they need a particular type of job, home or automobile to be happy. When adults adopt this type of mindset, they often make decisions based on their best interests rather than thinking about what might benefit society. This self-centered perspective illustrates how propaganda is a form of emotional pollution. To think further about this, it might be helpful to consider some ways to measure emotional pollution. Chapter Five explores ideas and strategies to do so.

Chapter 5
Measuring Emotional Pollution

Human emotions act as the foundation for emotional pollution. These internal sensations range from instinctive responses to multifaceted complexities described and labeled as happiness, anger, joy, sadness, guilt, hope, love and a variety of other terms. In most situations, when someone experiences discomfort and pain, emotional pollution is emitted to feel better. Those affected then exhibit similar types of behavior. While doing so, they produce additional emotional pollution. An example occurs when Frank and Jim are discussing a political issue. Frank expresses his ideas while Jim listens; Jim then shares his point of view. A verbal exchange occurs between them. At one point, Frank says something triggering an emotional reaction in Jim. Without realizing, Jim raises his voice in response. In turn, Frank also does so. As the conversation continues, Frank and Jim unknowingly pollute each other based on their level of discomfort felt at that moment. Their actions might range from immediately ending the conversation, to a physical confrontation. In between these extremes, are words used as pollutants. This example, like many other human interactions, demonstrates how the emotional pollution cycle continues just as it has in the past and will in the future.

The innate, environmental or combination of elements comprising emotional pollution can be further described using a burlap sack and brick example. Adults have a burlap sack attached to their back containing a variety of sized bricks. Some are heavy, representing adverse childhood experiences or ongoing toxic stress. While others, are much lighter pebbles of clay or shale symbolizing common annoyances. As a person's life unfolds, the content of the burlap sack changes based on the amount of emotional pollution experienced. For some, the frequency and intensity of pollutants significantly increase the weight of the bricks. This usually makes life difficult, as most actions are responses to feelings of fear, shame and guilt. Others have lighter loads to carry. Still, regardless of the weight of the burlap sack, emotional pollution plays a role in all decisions. Some of which benefit certain individuals and groups while harming others. This disparity in outcome leads to a culture where the majority determines their worth or value in comparison to others. It too perpetuates the belief in the pursuit of happiness. Emotional pollution however lessens the amount of time someone describes his or her internal sensations as happiness. A number of interrelated emotional pollution variables affect this state of being.

Sleep plays a role in emotional pollution. Without the appropriate amount, children and adults physically do not feel very well. This often causes them to emit pollutants in response to impulse-based assumptions and judgments about persons, places and events. A lack of sleep also increases and intensifies feelings of fear, anxiety and anger. These uncomfortable sensations normally result in emotional pollution that divide rather than unite people. From a broader biological perspective, sleep deprivation may affect how emotions develop and evolve over a person's lifetime. Parts of the brain influencing or controlling emotion might be adversely affected. This increases the emotional pollution associated with irritability, annoyance and disillusionment. These unsettling feelings contribute to ongoing difficulties with the sleep-wake cycle.

An individual's thought process determines the amount of emotional pollution experienced. The more concrete someone is the greater likelihood pollutants affect them. For instance, if adults have to directly experience something to understand it; they may be unable to identify a range of possible answers to questions. This narrow point of view makes it difficult if not impossible to be aware and sensitive to the needs of others. In contrast, adults who think more abstractly are resilient to the adverse effects of emotional pollution. For the most part, they can differentiate between what is and is not credible information. This ability causes them to spend less time thinking about the extreme points of view related to a topic. For example, they may accept as fact that the environment is in danger due to over population and global warming. They too realize the media's assertion that the "world is in peril" is an emotion-based headline used to attract viewers.

Individuals lacking food and shelter are vulnerable to emotional pollution. This results from believing information that is not always true. For instance, sayings such as "if you work hard, things will work out" or "this too will pass" are used to lessen discomfort and pain. In spite of these types of coping strategies, pollutants trigger thoughts related to survival. This mindset for some is so powerful it persists even when they no longer have to worry about their most basic needs. Many conversations continue to revolve around eating rather than a particular experience or an idea. Another economic related emotional pollution issue is the use of credit. The more someone spends money they do not have, the greater chance they can be misled. Examples are present in the banking industry. Many consumers are convinced they should be concerned about their credit score to gain the lowest interest rate possible on a loan. The credit score formula though is shaped if not designed by lenders. Clearly, the more financially independent someone is the less likely decisions are influenced by emotional pollution.

Emotional pollution leads to a number of outcomes. The most significant is how past psychological violations and anxiety about the future make it difficult to live in the moment. Instead, adults are guarded, hesitant to trust and communicate honestly. Thoughts and actions for that reason are skewed to some extent by subconscious or conscious attempts to avoid or escape discomfort and pain. Conformity is the natural outcome of this pattern of behavior. Individuals voluntarily relinquish a level of personal freedom and independence to feel a sense of acceptance and belonging. As this occurs, an invisible mask is worn to fit in with others. This form of self-preservation acts paradoxically; it helps to feel safe and secure while promoting dishonesty. Divisiveness rather than closeness is the usual consequence of these actions.

Emotional pollution affects a person's mood. This state of being is reflected in facial expressions revealing internal sensations, and by actions and reactions (Siegel, 2010). Those with a positive mood generally perceive themselves, others, and the events occurring around them favorably. They too are more likely to think with greater clarity and efficiency to solve complex problems. In contrast, adults having a negative mood are prone to view the world as ugly, demeaning and scary. These perspectives adversely affect judgment and sometimes result in isolation. Emotional pollution increases the amount of time with a negative mood. This is represented by the level of stress someone creates for him or herself. For most, stress activates physiological responses related to heartbeat, blood flow, metabolism, attention, and muscles. An example occurs when adults feel there are not enough hours in the day to get everything done. As this type of thinking develops, stress sometimes leads to a comprised immune system, an inability to maintain one's environment, difficulties obtaining a job or developing meaningful relationship. Adults experiencing these problems often emit emotional pollutants adversely affecting the moods of others.

Several things happen when emotional pollution creates an imbalance in moods. Those with an overly optimistic outlook view the world through the proverbial "rose colored glasses" or "the glass is half-full" perspective. This type of thinking acts as a protective barrier to negate or distort difficult feelings and thoughts. In contrast to this "happy go lucky" or "I am just happy to be alive" attitude, are those who have a "woe is me; the world is out to get me" mentality. Adults with this mindset often experience hopelessness, despair and self-destructive lifestyle choices. In spite of these differences in perspective, emotional pollution affects how adults react to isolated events. Many are dishonest about what they are experiencing while others make a "big deal" or exaggerate the significance of almost everything. It is as if the world is going to end if something is not done immediately. Ongoing emotional uneasiness also creates issues related to trust. With limited amounts, human relationships are difficult to establish, develop and maintain. Evidence of this challenge is the number of true friends someone has.

From a broad point of view, the culture is shaped by emotional pollutions effect on mood. This is reflected in human personalities. Freud (1938) suggested the id, ego and superego comprise personality. The id, the largest portion of the mind, is inherited and present at birth. It is the source of basic biological needs and desires. The ego is the conscious, rational part of personality that emerges in infancy to ensure the id's desires are satisfied in accord with reality. The superego, or seat of conscience, contains the values of society. Once the superego is formed, the emotions associated with ego redirect impulses so they are exhibited on appropriate objects at acceptable times and places (Freud, 1938). Emotional pollution intensifies the struggle between the id, ego and superego. As a result, all human beings to some extent are self-centered. This inability to think beyond your own needs makes it hard if not impossible for individuals and groups to work together to solve complex problems like extreme poverty, income inequality and violence. Self-centeredness as well reflects the frequency and degree in which children and adults experience fear. These uncomfortable feelings lead to a variety of actions described and labeled as bullying, discrimination, exploitation and sexism. Laws attempt to control these extreme reactions to emotional pollution.

All individuals experience emotional pollution. Therefore, this chapter provides information to think about how emotional pollution affects happiness. At no time is the content presented as a definitive answer to any individual or collective issue of concern. Instead, it is an attempt to measure something that has always existed but has been rarely if ever discussed. To begin, basic human needs are presented as the context to measure emotional pollution. Special emphasis is placed on establishing a link between need fulfillment, emotional pollution and happiness. Ideally, opportunities for broad societal change will occur if individuals become aware of emotional pollutions effect on happiness. If that were to happen, it might be easier to live in the world today.

Measuring Emotional Pollution

Maslow's (1943) hierarchy of needs is the theoretical foundation used to measure emotional pollution. He suggested physiological, safety, belongingness and love, and esteem are deficiency needs as they motivate individuals to act only when unmet. In contrast, self-actualization is a growth need. Adults attain it by developing their potential talents and abilities. The most important human need is physiological. Individuals require a certain amount of food and water in order to exist. If unmet, muscles begin to atrophy, the immune system becomes compromised, and eventually major organs no longer function. Physiological needs are also connected to emotional intimacy. In many situations, food is part of a social gathering to talk or celebrate a special event like a birthday, graduation or ball game. Children and adolescents in some families as well are taught to offer guests a beverage or meal, and if they do not partake when offered, they may offend the host. Other examples are present in the dating process. For some, an ideal date is dining at a restaurant or having a picnic in an idyllic setting. Another physiological need is sex. For most, physical attraction is the beginning of a possible relationship. As time passes, feelings of acceptance may lead to sexual activities. Having sex is not simply associated with procreation; it also results in a psychological response sometimes described and labeled as love. In many relationships, sex equals love, and without sex, emotional closeness does not exist. If individuals consistently meet their physiological needs, a positive self-image and an opportunistic outlook towards life usually develops. This demeanor leads to a sense of empowerment, a willingness to work with others, and a general belief that regardless of what is experienced; everything will eventually be all right.

Personal safety is another human need. Over time, words have helped fulfill this requirement. Children and adults gain a sense of security when terms are available to describe and label persons, places, things and events. An example is when a doctor diagnosis and explains someone's medical condition. This normally lessens fear and anxiety. In other instances, if acute or persistent periods of insecurity exist, instinctively, individuals avoid certain activities. Air travel is an example. Another strategy to promote personal safety is comparing your plight in life to someone else. Many feel better regarding the realities of their own experiences after observing the graphic images of violence in Libya or starvation in Rwanda. Emotional buffers and distracters also help to gain a sense of safety. Parents, guardians, and friends are the most common buffers relied upon when problems arise. Distractions on the other hand, are ideas and activities helping individuals escape difficult feelings. These diversions present themselves in a variety of ways such as the belief, individuals should establish goals to "reach for" or to attain optimal health adults should not work extended hours but rather participate in leisure activities. Despite the emotional comfort gained through language, avoidance, comparisons, buffers and distracters, many adults still struggle with personal safety. Collectively, this sense of uneasiness has led to the creation and enforcement of laws promoting a safer and more civil society.

Love and belonging are next on Maslow's Hierarchy. All individuals to some extent need to feel someone cares about them and they are a part of something. These feelings begin to develop when infants and care providers interact. In most instances, if adequate amounts of physical and emotional support are present, the child will feel loved. Then, as time passes, adolescents and adults usually gravitate toward others who are physically similar to them in order to gain a sense of belonging. If obvious commonalities are not present, they move in the direction of those with characteristics like family and friends who have provided them a sense of safety in the past. Once in shared space, communication patterns then act as the means for initiating, continuing and developing relationships. Common interests also play a role in love and belonging. When an individual talks with someone about a mutually valued topic, he or she increases the likelihood of obtaining positive internal sensations. This is evident when observing and listening to two men interested in antique automobiles. Their initial conversations focus solely on cars until they reach a certain level of comfort and trust. As this occurs, they sometimes transition from acquaintances to friends. For most, this increases feelings of love and belonging.

Esteem is another deficiency need. It consists of trying to attain strength, achievement, autonomy, competence, confidence, independence and freedom. Erikson's (1963) psychosocial growth theory describes how esteem develops. He suggested individuals experience eight crises throughout life. During the first or second year, parental nurturing and care determine if an infant trusts or mistrusts others. The second, autonomy vs shame and doubt, occurs between eighteen months and three years. A child decides if they are capable of doing things themselves or dependent on others. Toilet training is major defining activity. Initiative vs guilt occurs during preschool. "Am I good or bad" is the question at this point. Once children are old enough to enter school, issues related to industry and inferiority surface. Reading and math skills play a significant role in how young people feel about themselves. This ongoing self-esteem struggle continues as teenagers start to contemplate abstract ideas while simultaneously experiencing the crisis of identity vs confusion. Then, as young adults the question "Will I be loved or will I be alone" captures the dilemma of intimacy vs isolation. Decisions regarding marriage and children normally take place at this time. As adults' progress into middle age, generativity or stagnation becomes the issue. Contributing to society and doing things to benefit future generations are criteria to determine which perspective dominates. The final psychosocial crisis is integrity vs despair. The elderly reflect upon experiences to determine if they have had a meaningful life. Feelings of contentment influence their self-evaluation (Erikson, 1980). For some, a high level of esteem creates opportunities to fulfill Maslow's growth need, self-actualization.

Self-actualization consists of eight abilities. Concentration is experiencing daily activities fully, vividly, selflessly, with total absorption. Growth is the willingness to take calculated risks rather than relying on safe predictable patterns of behavior. Self-awareness means becoming more conscious of the inner self. Honesty refers to accepting responsibility for behavior rather than attempting to please others or to enhance your own status. Judgment is accepting and trusting feelings and ideas to guide actions. Self-development consists of exploring one's potential by living, working, and relating to the world rather than to a single event or accomplishment. Peak experiences represent periods of time when feelings, thoughts and actions are clear and accurate. Lastly, lack of ego defenses means to recognize how feelings distort images of people and events (Maslow, 1971). When individuals consistently demonstrate the aforementioned abilities, they reach the pinnacle of Maslow's Hierarchy, self-actualization.

Of the abilities comprising self-actualization, concentration is the most important. Concentration is the mental energy expended on an activity at a given point in time. Individuals require a certain amount in order to develop the skills needed to take care of themselves, work, and gain enjoyment from leisure activities. When someone has difficulties concentrating, intellectual stagnation is the usual outcome. With that being the norm, learning is limited to experiences in which a person directly participates. Fulfilling one's potential is difficult if not impossible when that is the case. A number of variables effect concentration. One is genetic differences result in some having the aptitude to focus for extended periods while others struggle to do so. Physical well-being is another issue. Children and adults lacking adequate food, shelter and sleep have problems with it. In addition, concentration is a developmental skill linked to attention span. The younger or more intellectually challenged someone is, the harder it is to teach him or her how to concentrate. Lastly, the number of daily activities an individual has to complete affects the amount of energy expended on each. For many, "there is simply too much to do to focus too long on one thing." This mindset limits opportunities to increase concentration skills. Without high levels of concentration, self-actualization is not likely to occur.

Human Needs and Emotional Pollution

Throughout life, people emit emotional pollution to meet their needs. This begins when infants cry to gain the attention of their parents. Then, once acquiring some words, children use them to influence others. As teenagers and young adults, most actions reflect an awareness of how certain behaviors are required to get what is needed or wanted. An example is the way employees follow explicit and implicit rules to maintain their job. Rationalizations are a more sophisticated form of emotional pollution. Many adults justify actions by making comments like, "It's just the way it is, and I cannot do anything about it" or "I do not have any other choice." Another less obvious illustration occurs in corporations. In some, a constant demand for increased productivity creates a culture where workers are afraid to lose their job. As these uneasy feelings permeate the employment setting, it is assumed, chief executive officers defend their policies and procedures by telling themselves and others of all the good they are doing by hiring so many people, generating local tax revenue, and improving the overall quality of life in the community. These and other similar types of thoughts and comments are emotional pollutants that help fulfill their needs.

The innate, environmental or combination of elements

comprising emotional pollution make it difficult to feel safe. These uncomfortable internal sensations trigger a search for some form of control. This normally occurs within the context of communication. It begins with a nonverbal message such as, someone's posture or eye contact. Sometimes, verbalizations follow. Other times, interactions end. However, if they continue, changes in voice tone, length of message, rate and word selection reflect the challenges faced while attempting to gain a sense of safety. These communication features can be conceptualized using various continuums. For instance, voice tone-soft to loud; length of message-short to long; rate-slow to fast, and word selection-ambiguous to explicit. The point in which an individual lands represents the extent of discomfort and pain felt at that moment. In most instances, emotional pollution results in actions closer to the extremes ends of the continuum. With that being the norm, ongoing issues related to personal safety sometimes manifest into anger, anxiety and a tendency to blame others for personal difficulties.

Emotional pollution is a barrier to feeling a sense of love and belonging. A number of reasons explain why this occurs. One is individuals create their own reality. This fluid characteristic of the human condition results in actions perceived as love by some and not others. Another, is how emotional pollution ebbs and flows. Children and adults are more vulnerable to pollutants in certain contexts at given points in time. Feelings of love and belonging as well play a role in how a person determines his or her value. This usually is reflected in emotionally loaded term such as, *self-esteem* and *legacy*. Emotional pollution also affects the level of agency and empowerment someone feels. The greater the frequency and extent of pollutants encountered, the less likely an individual believes they have control over the events occurring in their life. Lastly, adults who think and act differently than the majority struggle to obtain love and belonging. They are often alienated and targets of harsh treatment because of the discomfort they create in others.

The animalistic nature of human beings makes it hard to move beyond Maslow's love and belonging stage. For instance, basic survival instincts cause children and adults to be overly concerned about food. An extra refrigerator or freezer in the basement or garage provides evidence of this worry. Another example is how the human brain is hard-wired to remember negative more than positive experiences. This emotion-based reality intensifies the need for a sense of safety. It too leads to ongoing challenges in how children and adults perceive themselves. Psychological discomfort and pain also distort feelings of love and belonging. As a result, most contexts reflect the self-centeredness of people. An example is how societal disciplines like medicine, law and education develop their own unique language. To be part of the profession, someone has to spend vast amounts of time learning terminology, ideologies and theories. This form of indoctrination is reinforced by the emotional pollution associated with the belief that individuals should strive to be a part of something larger than them.

Emotional pollution influences the cultural definition of esteem. Today, esteem is connected to physical characteristics. Attractive individuals are viewed more positively than those who are unattractive. This is present in the experiences of Shannon and Jane. Shannon is a good-looking, well-proportioned youngster whereas Jane is overweight and ugly in the eyes of most. As Shannon and Jane enter school, teachers interact with them differently. In many instances, an instinct-based approach-avoidance dichotomy will result in Shannon gaining more attention, guidance and support than Jane does. As Shannon and Jane become older, an emotional pollution confounding effect will shape how each feel in relationship to the level of respect gained from others. Education level is another esteem variable. The higher the degree, the more status someone receives. Some professions like acting and athletics also receive greater prestige and levels of compensation. With that being the societal norm, most associate esteem with obtaining something or having certain abilities. This type of thinking often causes adults to emit emotional pollution while trying to gain symbols of success or developing highly valued skills. Those who struggle to do so are more likely to perceive themselves as weak, incompetent, and living an unfilled life. This mindset makes it difficult in not impossible to attain a sense of self-actualization.

The skills comprising self-actualization are shaped by emotional pollution. Self-actualization therefore is a relative concept based on the definition and evaluation of abilities at a given point in time. An example is the way appropriate behavior is determined. Quantitatively, a bell-shaped curve represents what is acceptable and unacceptable. Appropriate behavior is that which sixty-eight percent of the population exhibit. Those who are two or more standard deviations from the mean are often perceived negatively, labeled, and in need of help. From a cultural perspective, the standardization of phenomenon provides order while simultaneously creating an atmosphere where growth needs are difficult to meet. Instead, a normative perspective hinders concentration-the skill required to develop the abilities associated with self-actualization. In most instances, when pollutants enter consciousness, cognitive energy shifts from the current task to a thought about the past or future. The frequency and extent this happens is based on feelings of discomfort and pain. Some examples are temporary and fleeting like paying too much for a new phone, while others are long lasting and intense, such as those related to the atrocities of war. Another barrier to concentration is the emotional pollution associated with being hurt by a loved one. Most become intellectually stuck or even paralyzed, unable to focus on anything other than what recently happened.

A number of issues arise because of emotional pollutions effect on concentration. Productivity is one. As a result, most employees spend a large amount of time each week working. In the United States this is reflected in the belief, a full-time job consists of eight hours a day or forty hours per week. An unintended outcome of this way of thinking is people are prone to "kill time" rather than maximizing energy on a particular task. Another consequence is the number of projects that begin, but are not completed. A lack of ability to finish (three-sixty) demonstrates how pollutants divert an individual or groups attention from a task. In some way, this adversely affects the human physique, as most people need to feel their efforts result in some tangible outcome. Employers at times also intensify and perpetuate the uncomfortable feelings by implementing insensitive accountability measures such as, time clocks, weekly meetings, employee evaluations and extensive paperwork. Personal relationships also depend on concentration. It is difficult to understand someone without the ability to listen for an extended period. Emotional pollution thus hinders the closeness felt between people. As a result, many adults suppress their feelings and ideas. This pattern of behavior often leads to a sense of loneliness, negative self-thoughts, ongoing struggles with self- esteem and an increased likelihood of physical ailments. Lastly, if someone experiences frequent and intense pollutants, they may never be able to concentrate at the level needed to develop the skills associated with self-actualization. This is the reason why so few people are self-actualized. It too explains why individuals and groups are unable to work together to solve broad societal problems like climate change, violence and obesity.

The fulfillment of human needs is the context to measure emotional pollution. Maslow (1943) indicated there are five categories of them: physiological, safety, love and belonging, esteem and self-actualization. The first four are deficiency needs; the fifth is a growth need. Deficiency needs motivate people when unmet. In contrast, growth needs do not stem from a lack of something but rather from a desire to develop as a person. Emotion more so than intellect determines if someone is able to meet their needs. As a result, pollution in the form of emotion occurs. These non-verbal, verbal, and physical actions help individuals feel better while at the same time creating discomfort and pain in others. Those affected then exhibit their own unique coping strategies. This emotional pollution cycle leads to a number of outcomes. Most of which are related in some way to feelings and thoughts about food, shelter, safety, love, belonging and esteem. A link therefore exists between need fulfillment, emotional pollution, and happiness. The larger the amount of emotional pollution experienced, the less likely needs are met, and happiness is felt. This idea guides the upcoming discussion of how to measure emotional pollution.

Mood and Emotional Pollution: The Dependent and Independent Variables

In the current academic exercise, mood is the dependent variable and emotional pollution is the independent variable. Moods are emotional states reflecting how someone feels at a particular moment or over a period of time. They consist of interconnected internal sensations labeled as anger, calmness, contempt, disgust, fear, envy, happiness, jealousy, sadness, surprise and a host of other terms. Historically, the terms *positive* and *negative* have been associated with moods. It is difficult though to measure how someone feels using this broad dichotomy. A more helpful approach is one considering gradations or degrees. Descriptive terms such as *slightly*, *moderately*, *severely* and *profoundly* provide a more accurate mood assessment. To think further about this concept, a number of cultural observations need mentioning. One is how people are innately scared of the dark. This is evident when considering how individuals react after a storm causes the electricity to be off. Other similar types of feelings arise when walking a dog along an unlit mountain path. In these instances, the autonomic nervous system responds by signaling possible danger. When that occurs, increases in heart rate and sensory acuity usually happen. What is also noticed is how the word *dark* is sometimes interchanged with *black*. Over time, people have become conditioned to associate black with something negative. Examples include a child coming into the house dirty-dirt is usually thought of as being black. The highways are unsafe to travel-black ice covers them. Black clothing is worn at funerals.

In contrast, light is something to not be afraid of; it should be sought and cherished. Statements such as "when crossing over to the other side you will see this wonderful light" or "there is light at the end of the tunnel" illustrate this point. The word *light* is also frequently linked to the color white. For most, white is pure, pristine and positive. Some examples are the beautiful cirrus clouds in the sky, a wedding dress, and the white picket fence in the American Dream.

Color naturally affects a person's mood. More specifically, the eye's retina converts wavelengths of light into electrical impulses that pass to the hypothalamus, the part of the brain governing hormones and the endocrine system (Wright, 1995). This process triggers complex physiological reactions, which in turn evoke a psychological response. In most instances, this multifaceted dynamic sustains or alters an individual's psychological state. An example is how some children and adults feel differently on sunny and cloudy days. The warmth associated with sunlight promotes a more positive mood. In contrast, consecutive days of dark gloomy skies have an opposite effect (American Psychiatric Publishing, 2013). Other environmental events altering mood sometimes include the sun rising and setting, a rainbow, wildfires, tornados, earthquakes and ocean tides. The ways in which light and color interact also trigger internal sensations influencing mood. For instance, when tree leaves turn into shades of yellow and red, certain feelings related to colder weather and the holiday season may surface. White fluffy snow as well elicits a sense of a new beginning as plants become dormant until the rebirth of colors in the spring.

Color can also reflect an individual's mood (Mollica, 2013). Red, orange and yellow are considered warm colors as they evoke emotions ranging from feelings of comfort to anger and hostility. In contrast, blue, purple and green are cool colors. They are thought to be calming, and at times, reflect feelings of sadness and indifference (Mollica, 2013). With these concepts in mind, Wright's (1995) Color Affects System provides the theoretical foundation to estimate emotional pollutions effect on mood. Her research focuses on the psychological properties of the colors red, yellow, blue and green; and, the difference tonal variations and combinations of specific shades make in achieving visual harmony and psychological effect. Wright also identified eleven basic colors that are universal, regardless of shade, tone and tint. Each potentially has positive or negative effects relating to the human spirit, mind, body and the essential balance between them. Table One lists the eleven basic colors and their psychological properties (Wright, 1995).

Table One: Eleven Basic Colors and Their Psychological Properties

Color	Psychological Properties
Red	Positive: Physical courage, strength, warmth, energy, basic survival, stimulation and excitement Negative: Defiance and aggression
Blue	Positive: Intelligence, communication, trust, efficiency, logic, coolness, reflection and calm Negative: Coldness, aloofness, lack of emotion and unfriendliness

Yellow	Positive: Optimism, confidence, friendliness and creativity
	Negative – Irrationality, fear, emotional fragility, depression, anxiety and suicide
Green	Positive – Harmony, balance, refreshment, universal love, rest and peace
	Negative – Boredom, stagnation and blandness
Violet	Positive – Spiritual awareness, luxury, quality, containment and authenticity
	Negative – Introversion, inferiority, decadence and suppression
Orange	Positive – Physical comfort, food, warmth, security and fun
	Negative – Deprivation, frustration, immaturity and frivolity
Pink	Positive – Physical tranquility, nurture, warmth, femininity, love and sexuality
	Negative – Inhibition, physical weakness and emasculation
Grey	Positive – Psychological neutrality
	Negative – Lack of confidence, depression, hibernation and lack of energy
Black	Positive – Sophistication, glamour, security, efficiency and substance
	Negative – Oppression, coldness, menace and heaviness

White	Positive – Hygiene, clarity, purity, efficiency, sophistication and simplicity
	Negative – Sterility, coldness, barriers, unfriendliness and elitism
Brown	Positive – Seriousness, warmth, nature, earthiness, reliability and support
	Negative – Lack of humor and sophistication and heaviness

A few thoughts arise when reflecting on Wright's Theory. One is how the positive and negative psychological properties of some colors are described with words that could be considered contrasting or almost opposites. Brown for instance promotes warmth (positive) and lack of humor (negative). Can feelings of warmth occur without humor? In addition, words selected to describe psychological properties have subjective definitions. Examples are *heaviness, earthiness, coldness, simplicity, decadence* and *deprivation*. Lastly, color perception, preference, and meaning cannot be standardized as they are based on a combination of genetic, cultural and situational variables.

The Method and Process of Measuring Emotional Pollution

Basic color information is needed prior to describing the method and process of measuring emotional pollution. Color contains three components: Hue, Value and Chroma (Mollica, 2013). Hue is the overall color name. Value is the level of brightness. Colors with low value are darker (shades) and those with high value are brighter (tints). Chroma is the level of saturation. Colors with low Chroma look washed out. Others with high Chroma are bright (Mollica, 2013). An example is how pink, crimson and brick are all variations of red; each hue is distinct, differentiated by its Chroma and value. With this and other pertinent information in mind, five assumptions guide the use of color to represent mood. One is the relative nature of each hue. No color has purity in value and Chroma. Instead, technological advancements and the unique characteristics of individuals and groups determine how a color is perceived. Second, the internal sensations associated with a color are in some way influenced by genetic variables. Those factors cannot be easily identified. Third, color preferences are usually based on emotional experiences with them over time (Palmer & Schloss, 2010). The more enjoyment an individual receives from an object of a particular color, the more likely they like the color. Fourth, it is impossible to determine if genetic or environmental variables have a greater effect on the perception of color. A combination of inter-related factors seems more likely. Fifth, emotional pollution affects the value and Chroma of a hue. The extent in which this occurs is based on the frequency and intensity of emotional pollution experienced.

With these assumptions in mind, The RYB Color Wheel was used to select colors representing a person's mood. Painters, artists and designers rely on it to organize hues around a circle, symbolizing the relationships between primary, secondary and tertiary colors (Mollica, 2013). The three primary colors are red, yellow and blue. Secondary are orange, green and purple. Tertiary includes red-orange, yellow-orange, yellow-green, blue-green, blue-purple and red-purple. To quantify emotional pollutions effect on mood, each color was assigned a number based on the value and Chroma perceived by the author and a college student. Table Two is the colors and numbers.

Table Two: Colors and Numbers

Red	87
Blue	84
Orange	75
Green	71
Purple	62
Yellow-Orange	58
Red-Orange	49
Yellow-Green	45
Red-Purple	36
Blue-Green	32
Blue-Purple	23

Colors with a number of 50 or above indicate a positive mood; below 50 reflect a negative mood. The daily mood rating is documented in a hand-written or digital journal. An Emotional Pollution Perception Scale (EPPS) is then used to think about experiences affecting the color selected. The EPPS consists of two parts. The first is hourly time-periods to record events occurring throughout the day. A listing of social institutions where emotional pollution is most likely to happen comprises the second. Individuals reflect upon the descriptive data to estimate if emotional pollution in the family, places of worship, school or information from the media affected their mood rating. Criteria includes 1-not at all; 2-mildly; 3-moderatly, 4-severly and 5-profoundly. As this point, the self-awareness activity shifts to deciding if a plan of action will be developed to address the emotional pollution related to experiences rated a four or five. If yes, a discussion with a friend or counselor is conducted to explore new responses to the emotional pollution present in various contexts. The written plan of action acts as a tangible reminder and data collection tool.

At this point, a case study might clarify how to measure emotional pollution. Jack is the hypothetical participant. He is twenty-eight years old, single, a college graduate and a certified public accountant working for a large accounting firm. Initially, Jack has to make a commitment to learn and think about how emotional pollution affects his life. This appears simple but it is the most difficult step because of the discomfort and pain Jack may experience. He agrees to do so. To begin, Jack responds to a series of questions. They include do you compare yourself to others to determine self-worth? If so, how often does that occur? Are you seeking something tangible in order to feel complete? What might that be? Does the cliché, "it is greener on the other side of the street" sometimes reflect your attitude? Do you feel limited control over the things you experience? Are there specific settings where these sensations occur? Why might that be the case? Do you periodically reflect on daily experiences or the possible meaning of life? If not, why not? Answers to these and similar type questions provide baseline information to estimate how emotional pollution might affect Jack's thoughts and actions.

Next, Jack participates in activities to become more aware of his moods. To do so, he uses a hand-written or digital journal to record daily events and reflective thoughts. He also notes if a positive or negative mood dominated the majority of the day. Jack continues the process for a month. Now, he is provided information to help him identify gradations or degrees of a positive or negative mood. Jack documents how he feels in response to something seen on television, heard on the radio or read on social media. He is asked to think about why certain television shows are watched and not others. In addition, he is to identify the actions of characters leading to affective reactions. Jack then is given a series of questions to answer related to music and social media. An example is when listening to different types of songs, what internal sensations surface and sometimes linger? Another is why are certain social media sites viewed? As this introspective exercise unfolds, Jack is learning how certain stimuli trigger subtle mood changes in him. Then, at a more concrete level, he tries to identify the characteristics of people, places and events that result in similar types of feelings. Jack considers the obvious first; like smells, sizes, shapes, colors and personal mannerisms. He then reflects upon how multifaceted interacting variables like sunlight, voice tone, word selection and attitude might affect subtle mood changes. Lastly, Jack is to determine the extent in which his moods relate to core values. For instance, does he experience extreme discomfort (anger) when reading about a particular topic or observing a certain event? What may have caused him to feel that way? This self-awareness exercise provides Jack an opportunity to explore how emotional pollution affects his mood.

At this point, Jack's journal entries become more extensive. They include information about daily experiences, reflective thoughts, moods and emotional pollution. Jack uses 4x4 swatches of the thirteen colors and 3x5 number cards to help him identify and record his mood rating. After sixty days, the range of scores, mode, and mean are calculated. Next, a review of daily journal entries is conducted to determine if patterns in the data are present. Some variables considered include day of the week, time of day, setting, activity and people present. Emphasis then transitions to determining why certain types of feelings and actions are frequently recorded. Jack uses the Emotional Pollution Perception Scale (EPPS) to help him recall and record events occurring in his family, place of worship, school or information from the media influencing his mood rating. Knowledge of these emotion-based imprints on memory provides an opportunity for him to develop a written plan of action. The document focuses on teaching Jack new responses to try in situations previously creating discomfort and pain. As this transpires, Jack continues to monitor his mood and the percentage of time feeling happy. If desired changes do not occur, the sense of agency gained from doing something different may help him explore and develop other strategies to lessen the negative effects of emotional pollution.

Emotional pollution can be measured within the context of need fulfillment, mood, and happiness. A daily journal is used to record information regarding these interrelated variables. As descriptive data is gathered, adults become more aware of how emotional pollution affects their mood. These self-discoveries enable them to make judgments to continue or alter certain thoughts and patterns of behavior. If change is desired, plans of action focus on a series of incremental steps leading to some predetermined outcome. Each small gain is a self-awareness learning opportunity. Ideally, adults will spend more time happy than unhappy if they determine the frequency and extent emotional pollution effects their life. If that were to happen for the majority, the world might become a better place.

Chapter Summary

This chapter discussed how to measure emotional pollution. Maslow's (1943) human need theory was used as the context to connect emotional pollution with personal happiness. His five-stage model includes deficiency and growth needs. Deficiency needs motivate people when unmet. For instance, the longer someone goes without food, the hungrier he or she becomes. When food is obtained, individuals focus on gaining a sense of safety, then love and belonging, and finally esteem. In contrast, the growth need, self-actualization, does not stem from a lack of something but rather from a desire to fulfill one's potential. The skills comprising self-actualization are difficult to develop because of the emotional pollution associated with trying to gain a sense of love and belonging. These complex challenges provide evidence of the link between need fulfillment, emotional pollution, and happiness. The larger the amount of emotional pollution experienced, the less likely needs are met, and happiness is felt.

The chapter continued with a discussion of mood and emotional pollution: the dependent and independent variables. Moods are states of being representing how someone feels at a particular moment or over a period of time. Those with a positive mood generally perceive themselves, others, and the events occurring around them favorably. They too are more apt to think with greater clarity and efficiency to solve complex problems. In contrast, adults having a negative mood often view the world as ugly, demeaning and scary. These perspectives adversely affect judgment and sometimes result in isolation. Emotional pollution increases the amount of time someone has a negative mood. When that happens, individuals become more self-centered in order to feel better. As this pattern of behavior evolves, most if not all human actions act as fuel for ongoing emotional pollution.

The tools to measure emotional pollution were described next. The RYB Color Wheel was used to select colors representing moods. It consists of three primary colors: red, yellow and blue. Secondary is orange, green and purple. Tertiary included red-orange, yellow-orange, yellow-green, blue-green, blue-purple and red-purple. Each color was assigned a number based on its value and Chroma. A written or digital journal documented daily mood scores. An Emotional Pollution Perception Scale was created to determine how emotional pollution influenced the mood rating. It consisted of two parts. The first was hourly time-periods to record events happening throughout the day, and the second listed social institutions where emotional pollution is most likely to occur. Individuals reflected upon the descriptive data to estimate the extent emotional pollution affected their mood rating. Criteria included 1-not at all; 2-mildly; 3-moderatly, 4-severly and 5-profoundly. Emotional pollution plans of action were then developed. They contain specific goals and a series of incremental steps to alter thoughts and actions. A case study was presented to demonstrate how to measure emotional pollution.

Emotional pollution plays a role in everyone's life. For most, the innate, environmental or combination of elements comprising it results in thoughts about the past or future. As this occurs, innate talent, human diversity, and the beauty of nature are often overlooked. This inability to live in the present leads to self-centered actions to avoid or offset discomfort and pain. Granted, this happens as part of human survival; nevertheless, it has reached a point where broad societal change is difficult if not impossible. With that being the case, ideas, even if considered by some as folk psychology are needed to stimulate thoughts. This chapter has attempted to do just that by exploring how to measure emotional pollution.

Chapter 6
Ideas to Offset Emotional Pollution

The last chapter of the book discusses ideas to offset emotional pollution. To begin, readers are reminded that when individuals are born they enter an evolving, dynamic, and often confusing culture. Then, as infants, their family not only helps them survive but also begins to teach them how to live. As this acculturation process unfolds, children and adolescents are taught the importance of developing coping strategies for difficult emotions and thoughts. A number of outcomes arise from this. The most obvious is how human actions to some degree are self-centered. With that being the case, feelings of emotional closeness are limited. This is reflected in the statement, "Someone has had a good life if they can count on their hand five friends that would always be there for them." Another related issue is how it is impossible to be truly sensitive, empathetic or compassionate to others. Granted, some adults try to do so, but in actuality, many simply create and emit emotional pollution in spite of their positive intentions.

If people are present, emotional pollution is created and emitted. This characteristic of the human condition has led to the belief that external entities are necessary for fairness and justice to exist. In the United States, the executive, judicial and legislative branches of government play this role. Despite the founder's intent for separation of powers, emotional pollution continues to create an ongoing struggle between them. The basic human need for order is also present in laws. Without them, a large number of adults would struggle to function because of the fear and anxiety associated with the unknown. For instance, when a traffic light is not working, many are unsure as to what they should do. Emotional pollution also results in hierarchal structures where certain individuals receive elevated status based on family history, wealth, athletic or artistic ability, and education level. With that being the norm, a sense of envy and competition makes it hard to live in the present. Instead, individuals spend an inordinate amount of time thinking about the past or worrying about the future. They too often live in a "whirlwind" trying to gain something they deem of value. For many, this parallels a hamster running on a revolving wheel never going anywhere. Similarly, this is how some are in constant movement, much like ants in an ant colony. These types of behaviors reflect how emotional pollution is a societal constant.

The innate, environmental or combination of elements comprising emotional pollution are embedded in the human communication process. More specifically, children and adults use language to meet their basic needs while simultaneously creating and emitting emotional pollution. A number of reasons account for this. One is genetic and experiential differences effect how words are used. Emotional pollution is more likely to occur when words obtain multiple meanings based on the context they are spoken or written. Specialization, in the form of societal disciplines, contributes to the amount of emotional pollution present at a given point in time. As new discoveries are uncovered, differences in levels of knowledge lead to pollutants. An increased access to information further complicates matters. Many adults seem to think they know more than they actually do. This sometimes results in beliefs (mystics, parables and stereotypes) perpetuating ongoing emotional pollution. Lastly, words are a form of power. Those having an extensive vocabulary and understanding of language are able to influence others. Manipulation and control is a common outcome. This reality of life contributes to a variety of individual and collective problems.

Words are the most common form of emotional pollution. The reason is people vary in the way they use, interpret, and respond to them. An example is the terms *insensitive* and *disrespect*. What specific actions make a child or adult feel someone is insensitive to them? Is there a tipping point when the internal sensations associated with insensitivity become feelings of disrespect? By the way, how often does someone have to feel disrespected before he or she becomes angry and aggressive? The many possible answers to these and similar type questions lead to a variety of societal issues. Trust is one. The negative thoughts and actions associated with emotional pollution create an atmosphere of mistrust. With that being the norm, human interactions more often than not consist of surface conversations about jobs, the weather, or some sporting event. This reluctance to become emotionally vulnerable promotes acquaintance relationships rather than friendships. It too explains why acts of caring occur infrequently. Truth is another subject impacted by emotional pollution. What is perceived as true is based on the experiences comprising an individuals' personal story. For most, if new information does not fit neatly into the narrative, it is untrue. In response, children and adults usually conform to cultural norms in order to gain a sense of safety. This self-preservation strategy began when internal sensations were labeled a particular word. At that point, life became more complicated because no two human beings experience the same feelings. What someone might think of as joy is not the same for another. Naturally, this resulted in a number of emotional pollution related outcomes. The most important is its effect on human talent. Innate ability is more likely to remain dormant or not nurtured if someone is continually forced to conform. In addition, when feelings are standardized, adults are prone to view others as angry or in extreme cases mentally ill. Statements such as, "How can anyone have done something like that if they were in their right mind," make this point. In contrast, children and adults conform to be viewed favorably. By doing so, most believe they will obtain some desired lifestyle.

A number of questions arise when thinking about conformity. Is human existence simply part of an evolutionary process where an individual is born, has certain experiences, then they die and someone else takes their place? Do individuals live the same way as those who came before them? Are problems today like those in the past? The answer to these questions seems to be yes. The reason is, in spite of formal language and technological advancements, emotional pollution continues to shape and guide the level of conformity individuals' exhibit. For instance, regardless of the type of job, employees do things at times they are uncomfortable with to acquire money. Children and adults also willingly accept and follow rules. An example occurs when someone decides to walk to a neighborhood grocery store. As they leave their home, laws govern how they travel along the road. Once arriving at the store, certain actions are required in order to purchase desired goods. The seminal question then becomes; do children and adults develop a unique identity or do they conform to what the culture labels as identity? A number of thoughts arise when thinking about the answer. One, if a person is hungry or lacks shelter their real identity may not surface. In addition, if someone does not feel accepted, he or she might unknowingly sacrifice their individuality in order to be a part of some group. Lastly, without the necessary emotional support throughout life, adults are more likely to create an ego-driven false sense of self. Emotional pollution then becomes a response to the ongoing challenges faced while trying to become comfortable with yourself.

At this point, a few other things need mentioning before discussing how to offset the negative effects of emotional pollution. One is how human genetics determines the level of vulnerability to emotional pollution. Some individuals are more resilient while others are at greater risk. Another consideration is how emotional pollution is multifaceted. It is difficult if not impossible to identify and label a given variable as emotional pollution. Rather, it is an accumulation of a variety of evolving subtle factors adversely affecting thoughts and actions. In addition, from a human development perspective, no two adults encounter the same type and amount of emotional pollution. Instead, life experiences influence how emotional pollution affects their frame of reference. For instance, if someone suffers trauma at a young age they are more likely to experience emotional pollution then somebody who has not. Lastly, when individuals and groups try to help others, the concrete nature of human thought causes them to focus on custodial rather than emotional needs. This is evident in how donations for food, water and shelter occur in the aftermath of a hurricane or flood. In contrast, limited awareness and resources seem to exist for those experiencing less obvious conditions like depression and anxiety.

Ideas to Lessen Emotional Pollution

In the following pages, the intent of the author is to provide readers a few helpful ideas to offset the negative effects of emotional pollution. At no time does he believe the information is new or guarantees positive individual or collective outcomes. However, regardless of how rational or absurd ideas seem, they are something to think about for those interested and concerned about not only their life but also the experiences of others.

Emotional Literacy

The first idea to offset emotional pollution is to increase emotional literacy. The goal is to become more aware of internal sensations. To begin, readers are reminded that human emotions range from primitive reflexes to responses labeled as happiness, anger, joy, sadness, guilt, hope, love, and host of other words. These terms however oversimplify what someone feels. Emotions consist of dynamic, evolving, interconnected internal sensations unique to an individual. This complexity can be illustrated through an automobile example. While traveling on a busy highway, a dog runs into the road and is hit by a car. The motorist does not stop but rather continues to travel southbound despite being aware he struck something. In this situation, some onlookers become angry with the driver or blame the dog for being in the road, while others simply continue onward. A number of drivers also become so upset with what happened they contact the police or are willing to spend large amounts of money to help the dog. When reflecting upon this example, differences in responses to shared experiences point out a number of things about emotion. One is how early experiences in life affect current and future responses to environmental stimuli. If an adult had a pet growing up, they will react differently than someone who has not. In addition, if somebody does not emotionally respond like the majority, they often are thought to be abnormal or in extreme cases crazy. To avoid this, most people act like those around them. This lack of self-honesty is a major contributor to most if not all emotional pollution. Lastly, the emotion-based need for acceptance is a form of self-oppression. When children and adults have a strong desire to be liked, they voluntarily relinquish a part of their identity to be a member of some group. With these thoughts in mind, readers are encouraged to adopt the belief that emotions are neither good nor bad. They simply are internal sensations resulting from a combination of genetic factors and life experiences. For most, this new perspective will lead to greater levels of personal agency and empowerment. Individuals will experience less emotional pollution when this happens.

A written or digital journal is needed to become more aware of emotion. Initially, identify and document what is felt in response to scents, images and sounds. If possible, also note what internal sensations are associated with the words *happiness, sadness, anger* and *guilt*. To collect the information, reflect upon a few life experiences. For example, at a holiday party, why is a certain comment remembered years later and not another? Other questions might explore things that happened in school, the neighborhood or with friends and relatives. Then, after a few months of journaling, review daily entries to determine if patterns of internal sensations exist. By doing so, an increased level of self-knowledge may make it easier to uncover how emotion influences thoughts and actions. Next, record information you choose to include in your life. Discovering for instance why something is enjoyed might help to identify nuances in emotion. Variations in color, shape, texture, pitch, volume, rhythm and melody provide additional opportunities to explore internal sensations. Consideration should also be given to art forms. For instance, why does the Beatle's song, *Yellow Submarine* provide comfort after a stressful event or what is the reason a particular image results in a sense of happiness? Thinking about television and movie characters might too increase your understanding of emotions.

Another way to increase emotional literacy is to explore environmental stimuli triggering internal sensations. As animals, most if not all human feelings are in some way linked to survival. This begins when a newborn cries and continues until the end of life. In between these points in time, children and adults struggle to fit into a world often perceived as scary, dangerous and unpredictable. This reality leads to actions that provide a sense of safety and security. An example is how adults usually associate with those who look, think and act like them. Self-preservation is also reflected in someone's personality. More specifically, Freud (1938) suggested the human ego plays the role of balancing the pleasure seeking of the id and conscious of the superego. When attacks on ego occur, various uncomfortable internal sensations surface. Then, when these feeling repeatedly arise, many evolve into personal insecurities adversely affecting how someone feels about him or herself. These self-esteem difficulties often lead to ongoing challenges in the activities of daily living. Values are another less obvious trigger of internal sensations. When someone contradicts an individual's beliefs, it normally results in uneasiness and negativity. In addition, from a cultural perspective, the amount of emotional pollution present a given point reflects the ongoing collective struggle to meet basic human needs.

Now that you have become more aware of emotion and environmental stimuli triggering internal sensations, it is time to resume journaling. Concentrate on being as objective as possible while recording specific behaviors. Then, label and judge them based on some core value. An example is the desire to be helpful. Ask yourself a number of questions. Some of which might include: (1) what specific behaviors do I exhibit? (2) How frequently do I demonstrate them? (3) Are these actions helpful or hurtful to others or myself? (4) Do most of the behaviors promote closeness or isolation from others? (5) Am I generally happy with my actions? Answers to these and similar type questions lead to the next important self-awareness step. That is identifying and reflecting upon experiences shaping your view of reality. This will be difficult, as negative emotions will arise and often linger. Persevere, as the process will be empowering, as information will reinforce your current way of thinking or provide opportunities to alter your perspective.

Increasing emotional literacy will offset some of the negative effects of emotional pollution. Remember, emotions are neither good nor bad. They simply represent internal sensations reflecting who you are. Do not deny yourself of your humanity by conforming to what others think you should feel in a given situation. Instead, try to become more aware of the experiences shaping how you react to certain environmental stimuli. To do so, continue to write in a journal, compose music or participate in other art forms. Also, question why certain things are the way they are. Be prepared though for an emotion-based response (pushback) as some will become uncomfortable in your presence. Nevertheless, continue to search for answers, as it will help you uncover how emotion could be used as a catalyst to slightly alter or perhaps even drastically change some of the events occurring in the world today.

Communication

The innate, environmental or combination of elements comprising emotional pollution are present in the human communication process. In many if not most situations, children and adults subconsciously or consciously alter nonverbal or verbal communication to gain a sense of safety. A number of questions arise from this form of emotional pollution. For instance, are we treating someone with respect and dignity if we do not communicate honestly with them? How does emotional closeness develop if words are avoided that might create discomfort? In addition, can a person expect others to be sensitive to them if they are reluctant to say what they feel or need? Answers to these questions highlight how emotional pollution is usually in the form of words. An example is *love*. What one person perceives as an act of love may not be by another. Words with multiple subjective meanings reflect how emotional pollution evolves based on many complex interrelated variables. Some of which are communicated in families, places of worship, schools, and the media. Words also sometimes trigger internal sensations labeled as fear, shame and guilt. These uncomfortable feelings often lead to negative thoughts and actions that divide rather than unite people.

Honesty is another emotional pollution communication issue. Adults emit pollutants when they use words that soften or "sugarcoat" what is felt and thought. This results in some level of self-truth being lost, as individuals unconsciously skew their perspective in order to feel comfortable with their actions. Yet, for many, "deep down," uncomfortable internal sensations arise and linger. To overcome the difficult feelings, try to become more truthful. A suggestion is to lessen the frequency and amount communicated. It is not necessary to comment on some of the remarks made by others or respond to all digital messages. Instead, focus on linking communication to core values. A simple question to consider is does what you are experiencing matter in relationship to what is important. If so, communicate. Another idea is to become more direct. Say what you need to say and move on. Accept the fact you may hurt someone's feelings when you do so. In actuality though, you might be helping them by providing accurate and useful information.

Individuals emit emotional pollution when they do not understand something. This normally occurs as children and adults make assumptions about people, places and things in order to make sense of the world around them. Assumptions provide an immediate sense of safety and security while simultaneously limiting the ability to observe and listen. This leads to various forms of emotional pollution. To alter this thought pattern, reflect upon some of the experiences shaping your assumptions. While doing so, try to be open, observant, and objective. Openness implies being receptive, not clinging to preconceived ideas about how things "should" be. Observation is the perception of self within an ongoing experience. It places adults in a larger frame of reference and broadens their perspective. Objectivity is the ability to be aware that present feelings and thoughts are temporary. They are just mental activity, not absolute reality (Siegel, 2007). As this introspective process unfolds, prepare for many uncomfortable feelings. Continue though, as reflection provides an opportunity to gain information to reinforce or alter some of your responses to daily life events. This increased sense of agency and empowerment might also help to uncover answers to some of life's most important questions.

The pace in which someone lives effects the amount of emotional pollution communicated. If constantly on the go, pollutants are more likely created and emitted. This is due to individuals impulsively reacting rather than thinking before speaking or assigning meaning to what is heard. Two questions to consider regarding this matter are; what percentage of time are you in an emotional state that promotes thoughtful word selection, and how often do you fail to recall the content of a recent conversation? Answers to these and other similar type questions will result in an increased level of communication self-awareness. However, regardless of your current abilities, paraphrasing is a skill to develop. An example occurs when Bill and John are discussing gas prices. Bill states, "He does not understand why the cost of groceries continues to rise when the cost of transporting goods decreases." Bill continues talking about how frustrated he is after going to the grocery store. After Bill pauses, John then states, "did I hear you say, you think the price of groceries is not connected to the fluctuations in gas prices?" This type of inquiry often leads to clarification and greater understanding of the connotations related to certain words. It too provides additional opportunities for further dialogue. Some of which may strengthen the relationship between Bill and John. Another form of paraphrasing is asking what someone meant when using a word in a particular context. "Tell me what you mean by that" is an important question to promote mutual understanding. Emotional pollution is less likely to occur when that happens.

From a broader perspective, a state of calmness will decrease communication related emotional pollution. To obtain this, individuals should identify words and phrases triggering internal sensations. Terms such as *problem, hope, joy,* and phrases like "it is what it is" or were living in a "culture of fear" are some examples. Then, once you hear them, take a number of deep breaths while monitoring your instinctive reactions. Say to yourself, "relax and release" as you determine what you might say or do. This pattern of behavior will help you make the transition from the emotional (irrational) to intellectual (rational) self. Negative feelings and actions are less likely to occur when intellect dominates thoughts. Also, try to identify the link between words and experiences. An example is present in Shelby's life story. It begins in a home with parents who loved her but rarely expressed any emotion. Discipline was harsh, often hovering or crossing the line into abuse. Seldom did Shelby have the opportunity to communicate her needs and wants. These experiences resulted in an emotion-based sequence of thoughts as an adult. When experiencing something uncomfortable, Shelby labels the person or action as insensitive towards her. If the feelings linger and continue to be bothersome, the term disrespect enters consciousness. Some level of anger normally follows. As this pattern repeats itself, anxiety related to certain people, places and things cause her to create a great deal of pollutants for those around her. To alter this way of thinking, Shelby will have to discuss with someone experiences creating frequent and intense discomfort and pain. It will be difficult and hard. Her quality of life though will increase if she becomes more self-aware of how emotional pollution affects her interactions with others.

All behavior is communication. Therefore, the innate, environmental or combination of elements comprising emotional pollution is a societal constant. This historical reality is the reason why the concept of energy is important to consider. The collective expenditure of it comprises a person's life. The question then becomes are you spending energy in ways reflecting what is important to you? If so, or if not, what internal sensations make you feel that way? Readers are encouraged to accept that it is not a valuable use of energy to create, emit and react to emotional pollution. Instead, it might be more helpful to determine if a comment from a parent, sibling, teacher or coach has had a lasting imprint on memory. Does it in some way affect your quality of life? Also, remember you have an innate need for safety, acceptance and belonging. This often leads to various types of emotional pollution. To address these challenges, be more truthful. Say what needs to be said, and move on. Stop worrying so much about hurting the feelings of others. Rather, be present in spirit, mind, and body, as it will help you obtain a level of calmness needed to increase the amount of time spent in the intellectual self. This will result in positive rather than negative sensations dominating your being. As this occurs, feelings of happiness are likely to result.

Acceptance

Feeling accepted is a basic human need. In early civilizations, those who were, received food and protection from wild animals. Individuals not worthy of group membership fended for themselves, often dying. This type of thinking continues today in less obvious ways. For instance, if an infant consistently has their needs met, feelings of acceptance begin to develop. Actions of care providers then promote or hinder the frequency in which these positive internal sensations arise. An example is the time parents spend with their children. The greater the amount, the more likely a sense of acceptance surfaces and intensifies. Listening to a child or adolescent is another way to convey value. These early life experiences effect decisions in adulthood. Some of which promote happiness while others lead to sadness. An example is the process of falling in love. It begins when two people are physically attracted to each other. Then, one asks the other out on a date. Additional time together sometimes follows. As this course of events take place, a sense of acceptance acts as the foundation for feelings labeled as love. Without it, love is not possible. In addition, the greater the need for acceptance the more likely someone experiences emotional pollution in their relationship. This may be the reason why half of all marriages result in divorce. Another less obvious case in point occurs in an employment setting. If an employee feels accepted and valued, they are more productive and apt to remain in their current positon. If not, they often seek other opportunities. While in the process of trying to find a new job, their level of discontent might represent the degree of acceptance felt. This often determines the amount of effort put forth and time spent complaining or grumbling about their current employment situation. At a more abstract level, adults often choose to be a part of some group in order to feel accepted. These micro-cultures consist of those who share common experiences and beliefs. Today, the Internet provides a medium to locate and associate with various religious, civic, and interest-specific organizations.

A number of outcomes result from a lack of acceptance. The most obvious is a sense of rejection. These uncomfortable internal sensations often lead to a spiraling effect where one emotion-based action leads to another. For instance, adults who feel negative about themselves are prone to consume substances detrimental to their health, withdraw from others who care about them, or purchase items they cannot afford. When that happens, some experience a level of emotional pain that parallels a never-ending physical fight. To offset the difficult feelings, most try to avoid or escape certain environments. Many too develop psychological barriers or walls to protect themselves. An example occurs when someone has been lied to. They normally become more guarded when interacting with others to reduce the chance of being hurt in the future. Other common strategies to gain a sense of safety and security include comparing your life to others, rationalizing behavior, and, labeling and categorizing person, places and things. Each of these actions provides immediate relief. However, they do not address how to lessen the lasting negative effects of rejection on self-esteem. With that being the case, two ideas might be helpful. One is to make a list of positive characteristics you possess. Begin with broad terms like, caring, compassionate, loyal and fun loving. Then, note specific skills and abilities such as, athletic, artistic, analytical, listening and hard working. At the beginning of each day, perhaps at breakfast, read your list aloud and visualize the actions spoken. With time and repetition, it is possible to restructure neurological activity to become more positive. The second suggestion focuses on what to do when negative self-thoughts arise. Initially, try to accept them without instinctively reacting. A couple of deep breaths might help to do so. Then, decide the extent in which you want to spend energy trying to identify experiences shaping the negative feelings. Once determined, acknowledge the discomfort and pain associated with them. After that, try to let them go, imagine a balloon floating out of consciousness. It too might be useful to document the specific content of negative feelings and thoughts. By doing so, additional strategies might surface to address some of the challenges associated with self-esteem.

Adults who struggle to feel accepted often search for some form of control. An example is Sam. He is an office worker who feels his job is the only place where he has power. In a number of situations though, Sam is unaware of how others perceive him as rude and disrespectful because he is constantly trying to protect his company position and false sense of authority. What is also common is how Sam responds when someone requests to speak to his supervisor. His reaction usually reflects instinctive self-preservation behavior. The emotional pollution associated with a lack of control may also be the reason why Sam and other adults struggle with issues related to loneliness. When that is the case, many participate in activities they rarely enjoy simply to be with someone. As this transpires, individuals more often than not adopt the ideas of those around them in order to feel a sense of belonging. While doing so, it becomes difficult to identify and obtain their hopes, dreams, and desires. To offset this, think about the following statements. Loneliness is a natural part of life. Trying to avoid it is impossible. Loneliness reflects how previous experiences along with fear of the future hinder the ability to live in the present. Individuals are never alone as they have their own unique feelings and thoughts. With these ideas in mind, try to focus on emotional closeness in relationships rather than the quantity of them. Identify individuals you trust and enjoy being with. Spend time with them, and when opportunities arise, share your personal story. Remember to include a variety of positive and negative experiences. Feelings of loneliness will arise less frequently if you spend the majority of time thinking about others instead of yourself.

The relationship between pain, fear, and acceptance is another emotional pollution related topic. Pain is an unpleasant sensory or emotional experience associated with actual or potential tissue damage (International Association for the Study of Pain, 2019). Today, the perception of pain is different from the past due to technological advancements. Children and adults for instance no longer have to walk miles to locate a river or stream to wash their clothes as water and electricity are readily available in most homes. Other innovations such as automobiles, refrigeration, telephones, microwave ovens and computers have made life easier. In spite of these changes, people continue to fear pain. Pain however is a natural part of life. Therefore, being afraid of it or trying to avoid it results in emotional pollution. Pain is also not always negative; it provides information to stop whatever you are doing. For example, if your stomach hurts after eating certain foods, avoid them. Emotional pain as well clarifies core values. If you are disillusioned or depressed over some societal issue, it reflects something important to you. Perhaps, how some people treat others. At a more concrete level, a few questions might help identify how feelings of pain, fear, and acceptance interconnect. For instance, how often do you veer from daily routines (fear)? What level of safety and security do they provide? Do you rely on others to validate ideas (acceptance)? If so, do those individuals have elevated status? Is it uncomfortable to express your opinion in a group situation (fear)? Have you been taught to phone or text someone when upset about something (acceptance)? Responses to these questions provide valuable insight on how fear, pain, and acceptance interrelate. This information also provides opportunities to review how distractors and buffers might ease some of the emotional pollution associated with a lack of acceptance. Distractors are activities resulting in positive internal sensations. They might include meditation, a walk in the woods, fishing or some other activity. Try to identify and participate frequently in them. Buffers are people who consistently show they care about you. Share as many experiences as possible with these individuals. Focus on emotionally supporting each other. A pet may also serve as a buffer. Their unconditional love will certainly help to feel a sense of acceptance.

Emotional pollution lessens the amount of time someone feels accepted. The reason why this occurs is related to how individuals innately react to a perceived threat. For most, the sympathetic branch of the autonomic nervous system triggers a fight-flight-

or-freeze state of alert. This results in an increased heart rate, adrenaline entering into the bloodstream, and the stress hormone cortisol being released in preparation for the energy demands ahead (Siegel 2010). As this survival-based response evolves, it is difficult for someone to think beyond his or her own needs. This inability to decenter is the reason why acquaintances rather than friendships dominate most human relationships. Feelings of acceptance are less likely to occur when that is the societal norm. Self-centeredness also explains why individuals and groups continue to have difficulties listening and thinking about ideas different from their own. As a result, emotional pollution intensifies the need for acceptance. Some words like *Democrat* and *Republican* further exacerbate the issue by creating a competitive environment where individuals strive to be winners rather than losers. From a quantitative point of view, this decreases by half the number of people in which someone may gain a sense of acceptance. The link between competition and acceptance has too contributed to the creation of a class-based culture. This is evident in statements like "he is driving a Mercedes so he must be doing ok" or "they must be well off to afford a six-bedroom home with an indoor swimming pool." As adults strive to obtain social standing, high levels of stress lessen the frequency of feeling accepted. To overcome this self-imposed pressure, try not to determine your value in comparison to others. Instead, think about criteria for personal success based on outcomes related to spirit, mind and body. Doing so, may lead to less reliance on others for feelings of acceptance. Ideally, at some point in your life, acceptance will come from within. Once reaching this state of being, the negative effects of emotional pollution will occur less frequently.

Readers are encouraged to worry less about acceptance. Doing so will decrease the amount of emotional pollution experienced. To begin this life altering process, accept the fact various forms of indoctrination have influenced your desire to "fit in." This began as your parents taught you how to act in certain situations. Then, other social institutions like schools and places of worship reinforced the importance of conforming in order to be a part of a certain group. After reflecting upon these ideas, identify the degree you need to feel accepted. Ask yourself some questions. Start with appearance. Does your hairstyle or clothing reflect current trends? Another consideration is lifestyle. Do you strive to obtain certain things like the "American Dream" of owning a home with a white picket fence and a two-car garage? Think about family. Is it important your children attend a private rather than public school? Do extracurricular activities dominate family time? Now explore your perspective. Have you adopted the beliefs of your parents? Do you think and act like those around you? Answers to these questions provide valuable acceptance information. Then, make a value judgment based on the following statement. The degree in which I conform to societal standards to feel accepted results in more time being happy than unhappy. Your response provides an opportunity to think further about how emotional pollution influences your need for acceptance.

Emotional pollution affects the basic human need for acceptance. The greater the amount experienced the more likely life decisions are based on feeling accepted. When that is the case, children and adults emit pollutants as they try to be liked by those around them. Those impacted then respond in ways creating discomfort and pain in others. The emotional pollution cycle continues. It is possible though to alter the frequency and impact of this always present but rarely discussed characteristic of the human condition. To do so, readers are encouraged to worry less about being accepted. This change in perspective will be hard to accomplish. Nevertheless, adults are encouraged to reflect on social institutions influencing their thinking. For example, did your parents teach you to rely on others to offset difficult feelings or stress the importance of being a member of some group? If the answer is yes, ask yourself if it helps you experience more time being happy than unhappy. If not, review your level of conformity to societal norms for appearance, lifestyle, family and thinking. The information provides an opportunity to find a balance between relying on yourself or others to attain a sense of acceptance.

Identity

A person's identity consists of internal sensations, thoughts, beliefs and personality. It develops within the context of information processing. Information is acquired in distinct stages beginning with attending to a stimulus, followed by recognition, transformation into mental representation, comparisons with data existing in memory, assigning meaning, and acting in some way. More specifically, the processing of information begins with the sensory register, the first memory store (Snowman, McCown & Biehler, 2009). Its purpose is to hold for one to three seconds a series of sounds and images. If stimuli are recognized and then thought about, they will be processed and transferred to short-term memory. Short-term memory holds approximately seven unrelated bits of data for twenty seconds (Hambrick & Engle, 2003). Data is then transferred to long-term memory if maintenance and elaborative rehearsal activities occur. Long-term memory is an unlimited permanent record of everything an individual has learned (Schunk, 2004). This store of information is organized and summarized in abstract schemata. When these structures are well formed, and a specific event is consistent with expectations, comprehension occurs. If poorly constructed or absent, learning is slow and uncertain (Moreno, 2006). Emotional pollution plays a role in each stage of information processing. For example, if someone is experiencing pollutants, they frequently do not see or hear things; and, when they do, it is often distorted. When that is the case, adverse childhood experiences and ongoing toxic stress are more likely to occur because individuals lack information needed to develop important skills. These deficits collectively create a cultural atmosphere where emotion more so than intellect determines the information acquired and stored in long-term memory. Social institutions affect this complex dynamic.

Families influence identity. For example, parents who are authoritative provide rules and discuss reasons for them. As children demonstrate increased ability, they gain more responsibility. Youth living in these situations tend to be self-motivated, assertive, and able to work productively with others. Authoritarian parents on the other hand establish rules for behavior without explaining why they are necessary. This parenting approach promotes a lack of warmth and fosters resentment between the child and parent. In contrast, permissive parents provide little guidance and allow their kids to decide almost everything like what to eat, wear, and when to go to bed (Baumrind, 1991). Children with this type of parenting are markedly less assertive and usually lack fundamental cognitive skills. Similarly, rejecting-neglecting parents do not make demands on their children or respond to their emotional needs. They too often actively deny their parenting responsibilities. Immediate and extended family members also have an effect on identity. Siblings along with grandparents, aunts, and uncles' model and reinforce certain ways of thinking and acting. Family income as well plays a role in identity development. The larger the amount of resources available, the more likely a child experiences a variety of information and opportunities. Money is clearly not everything; nevertheless, it does influence identity. Emotional pollution is present in all families. The frequency and extent it exists determines the level of closeness felt within the family. Children and adults encountering pollutants are more apt to experience limited feelings of emotional support. When that is the case, survival-based thoughts usually dominate a person's identity.

Educational experiences affect identity. Two philosophical approaches have historically guided American schools: traditional and open (Skinner and Belmont, 1993). In a traditional classroom, children are relatively passive in the learning process as the teacher does most of the talking while students spend time at their desks listening, responding when called on, and completing assigned tasks. Student progress is determined by how well they perform on a uniform set of standards for their grade. In contrast, teachers in open classrooms assume a flexible authority role, sharing decision making with students as they work at their own pace to create knowledge. Student performance is evaluated in relation to prior development (Skinner and Belmont, 1993). Currently, in the United States, The Every Student Succeed Act of 2015 has led to a more traditional approach. This often results in students working silently and alone on skills measured on standardized achievement tests. Changes in school experiences have resulted from another educational trend: the inclusion movement. In inclusive schools and classrooms, emphasis is placed on building communities with everyone's gifts and talents recognized and utilized (Turnbull, Turnbull, Wehmeyer, and Shogren, 2020). Each individual is a worthwhile member of the group who has a role to play in supporting others to foster self-esteem, pride in peer accomplishment, mutual respect, and a sense of belonging. Two consequences result from this relatively new philosophical idea: class sizes are larger and vast learning differences exist between students. To offset these challenges, special and regular education professionals work in collaboration to design learning opportunities sensitive to all learners (Friend & Bursuck, 2019). This change in learning environment and professional responsibilities has created a great deal of anxiety and confusion among children and educators. Emotional pollution naturally results. When that is the case, students often lack the level of concentration needed to engage in increasingly difficult learning tasks. Concrete rather than abstract thinking is more likely to dominate someone's identity when that happens.

The media also plays a role in shaping identity. On a typical day, children watch television, listen to music, and spend time surfing the Internet. More specifically, Strasburger, Jordan and Donnerstein (2012) indicated youth in America spend nearly 40 hours a week accessing the Internet from their home computers. A number of reasons have been suggested as to why this is happening. Some parents are concerned about the safety of their neighborhood and do not allow their kids to play unsupervised. This results in them using technology to occupy their child's time. Another less obvious explanation is youth enjoy the physiological stimulation gained through animation and various levels of sound. Children and adolescents now also have the opportunity to gain access to formal education through the Internet. These programs allow students to learn at any time of the day and do not require travel to a specific educational setting. Information conveyed through the media plays a significant role in shaping identity. An example is how certain types of vocations like professional athletes, entertainers, doctors and lawyers receive elevated status. This contributes to the creation of a hierarchal structure in which adults strive to obtain some desired outcome. As this takes place, many adopt a norm-reference perspective where they determine their status in comparison to others. Judging the actions of others becomes a societal constant when this happens. The media also promotes passive rather than active thinking. In most cases, television programs do not stimulate thought but rather allow viewers to divert attention away from the mundane activities of daily living. Lastly, and perhaps most importantly, the media conveys images and sounds at a rate that promotes limited understanding. This is the reason why if someone has not directly experienced something, he or she has little awareness of it. Individual and collective difficulties are more likely to happen when this is the norm. These challenges act as fuel for the emotional pollution cycle. Those experiencing discomfort and pain exhibit actions to feel better while simultaneously creating problems for others. Now that social institutions have been briefly discussed, physical and cognitive skill development will be used to illustrate how emotional pollution affects human identity.

Physical appearance is the most obvious part of identity. Characteristics like skin tone, hairstyle, eye color, height and weight effect how someone feels about him or herself. Those positive about their looks have a level of confidence others may not. This normally results in opportunities for those perceived as attractive. Examples are noticed in television commercials. How frequently do see someone morbidly obese trying to sell a product? Have you ever witnessed an unattractive underwear or lingerie model? The desire to be attractive leads to various forms of emotional pollution. In some instances, adults strive to attain an impossible appearance. This often leads to self-criticism and a general state of negativity. Statements like, "I am so ugly," or "I cannot lose weight no matter how hard I try" make this evident. Personal relationships suffer with this mindset. For instance, jealousy and envy are present in statements such as, "they think they are better than I am" or "they do not work the long hours like I do, so they have time to work out." Feelings of unattractiveness also sometimes cause adults to isolate or congregate with others who look much like them. As this occurs, the emotional pollution associated with trying to gain a sense of acceptance creates an atmosphere of division rather than closeness.

Emotional pollution hinders physical development. This begins when children younger than two years old have decelerated or arrested physical growth associated with poor developmental and emotional functioning. Infants who fail to thrive have bodies looking malnourished and are withdrawn and apathetic (Gupta, 2014). These early problems sometimes lead to a comprised immune system. This increases the risk for various viruses, cardiovascular diseases, certain forms of cancer, and a variety of autoimmune disorders. Physical discomfort and pain also makes it difficult to fall asleep, stay asleep, and sleep deeply. Without enough rest, children and adults are vulnerable to the negative effects of emotional pollution. These difficulties have an ongoing detrimental effect on the billions of neurons comprising the human brain. As neurons form connections, emotional pollution acts as a barrier to the stimulation needed for their survival. Those seldom aroused and strengthened will die off. This dynamic, complex, and multifaceted process of neurological development provides the foundation for cognitive skills.

Piaget (1930) suggested cognitive skills develop in stages

characterized by qualitatively distinct ways of thinking. In the sensorimotor stage (birth to two years), infants use their senses to explore the world. They often invent ways to locate desired objects or obtain attention from those around them. These patterns of behavior evolve into the symbolic but illogical thinking of the preschooler in the preoperational stage (two to seven years). Language skills are beginning to develop during this time-period. Then, cognition transforms into the more organized reasoning of the school-age child in the concrete operational stage (seven to eleven years). Children are able to arrange objects into categories based on some identifying feature. Finally, in the formal operation stage (twelve years and beyond), thought becomes more abstract as individuals have the ability to identify options to solve complex problems (Piaget, 1930). Emotional pollution affects many aspects of Piaget's stages. The most obvious is the perception of stimuli. If pollutants are consistently present, an individual often misinterprets information and exhibits inappropriate actions. An example sometimes occurs when a child or adult feels insecure. They often spend an excessive amount of time and energy trying to gain a sense of belonging in order to feel safe. This may cause them to become stuck or incapable of moving beyond the concrete operational stage of cognitive development. Emotional pollution also limits intellectual growth. In many instances, if a child or adult feels harmed in some way by their parents, friends, teachers or employer, they are more likely to recall the exact events. In contrast, if they have a pleasant experience, they are less apt to remember what specifically occurred. This survival-based mentality makes it difficult to transition from concrete to abstract thinking.

Emotional pollution acts as a barrier to cognitive development. An example is noticed when Billy, a fourth grader, participates in cooperative group activities. He struggles to concentrate during the lesson because other students have laughed at him in the past or the teacher has made him feel as though he is incapable. Billy's inability to learn at that particular moment might ultimately result in difficulties understanding things he has not directly encountered. This type of thinking may cause him to exhibit adolescent-type behavior as an adult. For others, frequent and intense periods of emotional pollution cause them to be paralyzed, unable to increase their cognitive skills. This often occurs when a soldier is deployed to a war zone. In spite of their family members' strong desire to succeed in college, worry may limit their ability to attain the level of concentration needed to acquire, comprehend, and retain new information.

Human interactions also affect cognitive development. Nonverbal and verbal messages however often do not promote understanding. Instead, they create confusion, discomfort and a host of other issues. As a result, emotional pollution limits intellectual curiosity. To think further about this, it might be fun to personify talent. The talent within someone is shouting, "Help me, help me, I can't get out." After a while, it becomes angry, disillusioned and sad, and ultimately remains dormant and dies. To change this sequence of events, readers should accept things as they unfold. In most instances, the more you hope, wish or force something to happen, the less likely it is to occur. Certain things regardless of specific actions simply come about. For example, when a tornado touches the ground, no explanation can be provided as to why some houses in a neighborhood are devastated and others are spared. If individuals would just let things naturally evolve, they might also become more sensitive to others in different circumstances than their own. If that would happen, a learning opportunity personal perspective might develop where adults realize they can learn something from everyone. This mindset increases the chance someone might uncover and nurture their innate cognitive abilities.

Emotional pollution affects physical and cognitive development. As this characteristic of the human experience unfolds, individuals might experience happiness more frequently if they would not take themselves so seriously. The world will exist regardless if you are present or not. To think about this travel somewhere you have spent a significant amount of time in the past. What do you observe? Some trees perhaps are gone or become larger, parks renamed, and the city population may have shifted to a different part of the town. Now, purchase a local newspaper. Has the content changed much? Are there still reports of crime, self-help columns and articles describing programs trying to assist the less fortunate or protect the environment? Answers to these questions probably are yes. So, why then do most people personalize the events happening around them? Emotional pollution is the reason. Pollutants create a level of discomfort and pain that result in some constant state of self-preservation. As this occurs, the human ego acts to buffer the uncomfortable feelings while also simultaneously hindering possibilities for growth. An example is how some individuals believe they are incapable or powerless to determine their fate. This type of thinking hinders their quality of life. Possibilities for change however do exist. To begin, try to determine how often you think about yourself. Writing in a journal might help uncover your level of self-centeredness. Slowing down to enjoy the moment is another suggestion. What are some of the smells, sounds, and images you are experiencing? Also, try not to be so judgmental, just experience what it is. Lastly, and perhaps most difficult, is to not be fearful of death. Try to live in the present, expending energy in ways reflecting what is important to you and those whom you love. Remember, emotional pollution influences your energy expenditure to the extent in which you allow it. When in doubt, laugh at yourself, as it will help you remember to take yourself less seriously.

Another identity consideration is to accept your own ignorance. Regardless of genetic endowment and personal experiences, it is impossible to be knowledgeable on many things. Stop pretending you know more than you do. Accepting this fact will allow you to create your own unique path in life rather than doing what others think you should. It is your life, not theirs. Also, conform less as you try to identify persons, places and things that allow you to spend more time being happy than unhappy. To do so, think about internal sensations. How do they feel? What emotions do you assign them? Remember, emotions are neither good nor bad. They simply represent your present state of humanity. In reality though, the accumulation of negative feelings result in personal insecurities-warts (Ruediger, 2014). Try to identify them. To do so, use a timeline approach consisting of childhood, school-aged, adolescence, early, middle and late adulthood. Think about some of the experiences that led to feelings of fear, sadness, joy, and happiness. Ask yourself how emotional pollution influenced what you remember. This process will be hard; however, it provides an opportunity to accept what you do and do not know. Self-truth promotes a higher quality of life.

Emotional pollution affects human identity. This occurs within the context of information processing. The pollutants experienced in family, school, places of worship and media have an effect on how an individual attends to and recognizes stimuli, assigns meaning, and stores information to guide future actions. When emotional pollution is present, environmental stimuli is often unnoticed or when it is, it is distorted by feelings of discomfort and pain. This results in a number of identity related issues. The most obvious is limited knowledge. Without being aware and understanding certain things, high levels of anxiety may make it difficult to sleep. Children and adults experiencing this often lack the level of concentration needed to develop and use abstract thinking abilities. When that is the case, many conform to societal standards for thoughts and actions. This usually results in adults adopting a norm-referenced perceptive where personal worth and value is determined in comparison to others. Jealousy, envy and anger often arise when this cultural atmosphere exists. These uncomfortable feelings also increase the chance a survival mentality dominates a person's identity. Frequent and intense emotional pollution is more likely to occur when this happens.

Chapter Summary

The problems occurring throughout the world today are caused by the innate, environmental or combination of elements comprising emotional pollution. It is difficult however to identify and label something as emotional pollution. Rather, it is a multifaceted accumulation of a variety of evolving subtle factors negatively affecting thoughts and actions. From a human development perspective, certain children and adults are more resilient to pollutants while others are at greater risk. Individuals as well do not encounter the same type and amount of emotional pollution. Instead, past and current life experiences determine how pollutants affect their frame of reference. The concrete nature of most thoughts also results in adults being unaware of emotional pollution. This is the reason why it continues today just as it has in the past.

This chapter presented ideas to offset emotional pollution. Increasing emotional literacy was the first suggestion. Readers were encouraged to write in a journal, compose music or participate in other art forms to identify how internal sensations influence their responses to environmental stimuli. While doing so, they were urged to rethink their perspectives on emotion. Emphasis was placed on adopting the belief that emotions are neither good nor bad. They simply represent an important part of one's humanity. This change in mindset would result in less emotional pollution. Communication was the next topic discussed. To some degree, emotional pollution is a constant within the communication process. Words are the major sources of pollutants, especially those having multiple meanings. To lessen emotional pollution, adults need to be more direct when interacting with others. Say what needs to be said, and move on. Stop being so concerned about hurting someone's feelings. Instead, try to be present in spirit, mind, and body, as it will help to attain a level of calmness needed to communicate in ways promoting emotional closeness.

The basic human need for acceptance was then explored. This psychological requirement affects many life decisions. Some of which promote happiness while others lead to sadness. Children and adults should worry less about being accepted. This will be difficult to accomplish as many social institutions stress the importance of "fitting in". Nevertheless, adults should reflect on how family, school, places of worship and the media have influenced their thinking. The information uncovered might help to find a balance between relying on yourself or others to attain the sense of acceptance needed to feel happy. Ideally, at some point in life, acceptance will come from within. Once reaching this state of being, the negative effects of emotional pollution will occur less frequently.

The chapter ends with a discussion of human identity. A person's qualities, beliefs and personality develop within the context of information processing. With that being the case, emotional pollution determines the degree in which an individual has a fear-based identity. To feel safe and more secure in daily activities, adults should take themselves less seriously. Not everything is about you. Another related identity consideration is to accept your own ignorance. Stop pretending you know more than you do. Acknowledging this truth will allow you to create your own unique path in life rather than doing what others think you should. In addition, conform less to cultural standards for appearance, lifestyle, and personal perspective. This will help you gain the level of agency and empowerment needed to increase feelings of happiness.

Individual and collective change is possible. It will only happen though when people are aware of emotional pollution and its effect on thoughts and actions. If that were to occur, children and adults would be more likely to experience positive internal sensations labeled as happiness. This increase in positive energy would result in a culture where more opportunities exist to identify and nurture human talent. Some of which might act as catalysts to address the many complex issues related to extreme poverty, gun violence, inequality and a host of other societal concerns. It will become easier to live in the world if people emitted less emotional pollution. A societal constant rarely discussed.

Content Review

The following is a list of the major ideas presented in *Emotional Pollution: Always present but rarely discussed*.

- Emotion rather than intellect guides most human actions.
- Emotional pollution results from uncomfortable internal sensations.
- Individuals create and emit emotional pollution to lessen feelings of discomfort and pain.
- Emotional pollution is the innate, environmental or combination of elements negatively affecting thoughts and actions.
- Emotional pollution makes it difficult to live in the present.
- Communication is the context where emotional pollution most frequently occurs.
- Families, schools, places of worship and the media influence the characteristics of emotional pollution.
- Propagandists strategically use emotional pollution for personal gain.
- Emotional pollution plays a major role in individual and collective decisions.
- Emotional pollution is the reason why world problems exist.
- The frequency and extent of emotional pollution experienced affects the amount of time someone is happy or unhappy.
- Emotional pollution is the reason why people treat each other badly.

- Individual and collective moods are a possible way to measure emotional pollution.

- It is possible to decrease the amount of emotional pollution experienced.

- Emotional literacy, communication, acceptance, and identity are topics to think about when exploring ways to lessen emotional pollution.

- It would be easier to live in the world if people emitted less emotional pollution.

References

Akerlof, G. A. & Shiller, R. J. (2009). *Animal spirits: How human psychology drives the economy and why it matters for global capitalism*. Princeton, NJ: Princeton University Press.

American Psychiatric Publishing. *(2013). Diagnostic and statistical manual of mental disorders: DSM-5. Washington (D.C.).*

Baumrind, D. (1991). Parenting styles and adolescent development. In R. M. Lerner, A. C., Peterson, Brooks-Gunn (Eds.), *Encyclopedia of adolescence*. New York, NY: Garland Publishing.

Baumrind, D. (2005). Patterns of parental authority and adolescent authority. *New Directions for Child and Adolescent Development*, 108, 61-69.

Beatles (1969). *Yellow Submarine*. Hollywood: Apple Records

Bronfenbrenner, U. (1979). *The ecology of human development: Experiments by nature and design*. Cambridge, MA: Harvard University Press.

Bronfenbrenner, U. (1995). The bio-ecological model from a life course perspective: Reflections of a participant observer. In P. Moen, G. H. Elder Jr., and K. Luscher (Eds.), *Examining lives in context* (pp. 599–618). Washington, DC: American Psychological Association.

Bronfenbrenner, U. (1997). *The ecology of developmental processes.* In R. M. Lerne (Ed.), *Handbook of child psychology: Theoretical models of human development.* New York, NY: Wiley.

Dawkins, R. (1976). *The selfish gene.* Oxford, UK: Oxford University Press.

Debos, R. (1969). So *human an animal.* New York, NY: Charles Scribner's Sons.

Dyson, M. E. (2007). *Know what I mean: Reflections on Hip Hop.* New York, NY: Basic Books.

Ellison, R. (1952). *Invisible man.* New York, NY: Random House.

English Standard Version Bible, 2001, Ex. 20:2-17.

Erikson, E. H, (1962). *Childhood and society* (2nd ed.). New York, NY: W. W. Norton & Company.

Erikson, E. H. (1980). *Identity and the life cycle* (2nd ed.). New York, NY: W. W. Norton & Company.

Freud, S. (1933). *Introductory lectures on psychoanalysis* (The Standard Edition). New York, NY: W.W. Norton & Company.

Freud, S. (1938). *An outline of psychoanalysis.* London, England: Hogarth.

Friend, M. & Bursuck, W. D. (2019) *Including students with special needs: A practical guide for classroom teachers* (eight ed.). Boston, MA: Pearson.

Fugate, J. M. B. & Franco, C. L. (2019). What color is your anger? Assessing color-emotion pairings in English speakers. *Frontiers in Psychology*, 10:206.

Gates, H. L. Jr. & West, C. (1996). *The future of the race*. New York, NY: Alfred A. Knopf.

Griffin, L. (2016). McLane Dothan is expanding its grocery distribution center. *Dothan Eagle*: Dothan, Alabama.

Gupta, R. C. (2014). Failure to thrive. https://kidshealth.org/en/parents/failure-thrive.html retrieved August 19, 2019.

Hambrick, D. Z. & Engle, R. W. (2003). The role of working memory in problem solving. In J. E. Davidson & R. J. Stenberg (Eds.). *The psychology of problem solving* (pp. 176-205). Cambridge, England: Cambridge University Press.

Harrub, B., Thompson, B., & Miller, D. (2003). The origin of language and communication. *Journal of Creation*, *17*(3), 93-101.

Hartmann, D. (2016). *Midnight basketball: Race, sport, and neoliberal social policy*. Chicago, IL: The University of Chicago Press.

Hoffman, M. L. (2000). *Empathy and Moral Development*. New York, NY: Cambridge University Press.

International Association for the Study of Pain. https://www.iasp-pain.org/ retrieved August 20, 2019

Jahnayi, N. (2020). Eight Types of Adjectives with Examples to Learn Their Use retrieved May 10, 2020 https://www.englishbix.com/types-of-adjectives-with-examples-use/

Kaiser Family Foundation (2010). Generation M2 – Media in the lives of 8 – 18 year olds. http://kaiserfamilyfoundation.files.wordpress.com/2013/01/8010.pdf. Retrieved August 19, 2019.

Ketcham, H. (2017, March 30). 'Dennis the Menace' [Cartoon] *Dothan Eagle*: Dothan, AL. p. 5B.

Kuhn, T. (1962). *Structure of scientific revolutions* (1st Ed.). Chicago, IL: University of Chicago Press Lasswell, H. D. (1965). *World politics and personal insecurity*. New York, NY: The Free Press.

Lasswell, H. D. (1971). *Propaganda technique in World War I*. Cambridge, MA: The M.I.T. Press.

Lewis, J. & Jones, B. (2012). *Across that bridge: Life lessons and a vision for change*. New York, NY: Hachette Books.

Maslow, A. H. (1943). *A theory of human motivation*. Psychological Review, 50 (4), 370–396.

Maslow, A. H. (1968). *Toward a psychology of being* (2nd ed.). Princeton, NJ: Van Nostrand.

Maslow, A. H. (1971). *The farther reaches of human nature*. New York, NY: Penguin Random House Books.

Merriam-Webster. (n. d.) Assumptions. In Merriam-Webster.com dictionary. Retrieved November 8, 2016, from https://www.meriam-webster.com/dictionary/assumptions.

Merriam-Webster. (n. d.) Caring. In Merriam-Webster.com dictionary. Retrieved November 10, 2016, from https://www.meriam-webster.com/dictionary/caring.

Merriam-Webster. (n. d.) Contentment. In Merriam-Webster.com dictionary. Retrieved November 20, 2016, from https://www.meriam-webster.com/dictionarycontentment.

Merriam-Webster. (n. d.) Guilt. In Merriam-Webster.com dictionary. Retrieved November 22, 2016, from https://www.meriam-webster.com/dictionary/guilt.

Merriam-Webster. (n. d.) Selfish. In Merriam-Webster.com dictionary. Retrieved November 30, 2016, from https://www.meriam-webster.com/dictionary/selfish.

Merriam-Webster. (n. d.) Table. In Merriam-Webster.com dictionary. Retrieved November 12, 2016, from https://www.meriam-webster.com/dictionary/table.

McWhorter, J. (1998). *The word on the street: The fact and fable about American English.* New York, NY: Plenum Trade.

McWhorter, J. (2000). *Losing the race: Self-sabotage in Black America.* New York, NY: Simon & Schuster.

Mollica, P. (2013). *Color theory: An essential guide to color from basic principles to practical application.* Laguna Hills, CA: Walter Foster Publications.

Moreno, R. (2006). Learning in high-tech and multimedia environments. *Current Directions in Psychological Sciences*, 15 (2), 63-67.

Palmer, S. E., Schloss, K. B. (2010). An ecological valence theory of human color preference. *Proceedings of the National Academy of Sciences*, 107 (19), 8877-8882.

Piaget, J. (1930). *The child's conception of the world.* New York: Harcourt, Brace & World.

Pinker, S. (1995). *The language instinct.* New York, NY: Harper Perennial.

Pinker, S. (2002). *The blank slate: The modern denial of human nature.* New York, NY: Penguin Putnam Inc.

Pinker, S. (2007). *The stuff of thought: Language as a window into human nature.* New York, NY: Penguin Putnam Group.

Plamper, J. (2015). *The history of emotions: An introduction.* United Kingdom: Oxford University Press.

Rosenwein, B. H. (2006). *Emotional communities in the Early Middle Ages.* Ithaca, NY: Cornell University Press.

Ruediger, G. (2014). *People: Is real change possible?* Mustang, OK: Tate Publishing and Enterprises, LLC.

RYB Color Wheel n.d., w3schools.com retrieved January 14, 2020.

S 1177 The Every Student Succeeds Act (2015). Pub. L 114-95.

Schunk, D. H. (2004). *Learning theories: An educational perspective* (4th ed.). Upper Saddle River, NJ: Merrill Prentice Hall.

Siegel, D. J. (1999). *The developing mind: Toward a neurobiology of interpersonal experience.* New York, NY: Guilford.

Siegel, D. J. (2007). *The mindful brain: Reflection and* attunement *in the cultivation of well-being.* New York, NY: W. W. Norton & Company.

Siegel, D. J. (2010) *Mindsight: The new science of personal transformation.* New York, NY: Bantam Books.

Skinner, E. A., & Belmont, M. J. (1993). Motivation in the classroom: Reciprocal effects of teacher behavior and student engagement across the school year. *Journal of Educational Psychology, 85,* 571-581.

Smith, A. (1776). *Wealth of nations.* New York, NY: P.F. Collier & Sons. Snowman, J., McCown, R., & Biehler, R. (2009). *Psychology applied to teaching* (12th ed.). Boston, MA: Houghton Mifflin Company.

Strasburger, V. C., Jordan, A. M. & Donnerstein, E. (2012) Children, adolescents, and the media: Health effects. *Pediatric Clinics of North America, 59,* 533-587.

Turnbull, A., Turnbull, R., Wehmeyer, M. L., & Shogren, K. A. (2020). *Exceptional Lives: Practice, progress, & dignity in today's schools* (9th edition). Hoboken, NJ: Pearson.

United States Environmental Protection Agency (2014). Washington, D. C. http://www.epa.gov/ Wright, A. (1995). *The beginner's guide to color psychology.* London, UK: Kyle Cathic Limited.

Young, P. T. (1943). *Emotion in man and animal: Its nature and relation to attitude and motive.* New York: John Wiley & Sons.

www.ingramcontent.com/pod-product-compliance
Lightning Source LLC
Chambersburg PA
CBHW071445070526
44578CB00001B/220